A Practical Guide to Rational Emotive Behavioural Coaching

In his clear and concise style, Windy Dryden outlines the steps and strategies that coaches using Rational Emotive Behavioural Coaching (REBC) should employ as a guide when working with coachees in development-focused REBC and in problem-focused REBC (addressing both practical and emotional problems).

A Practical Guide to Rational Emotive Behavioural Coaching shows how REB coaches can address the inevitable obstacles to coaching progress that are likely to occur in all types of REBC and outlines the most common steps for each type of coaching, including common strategies for the implementation of each step. The book also includes a unique survey, developed by the author, designed to help coachees in development-focused REBC assess and evaluate healthy principles of living.

The book will be an essential resource for coaches in practice and training, for professionals working in human resources and learning and development, and for executives in a coaching role.

Windy Dryden, PhD, is in part-time clinical and consultative practice and is an international authority on cognitive behaviour therapy (CBT). He is Honorary Vice President of the International Society for Coaching Psychology, was granted honorary membership in the International Association of Cognitive-Behavioral Coaching in 2014 and is Emeritus Professor of Psychotherapeutic Studies at Goldsmiths University of London. He has worked in the helping professions for more than 40 years and is the author and editor of over 220 books.

Routledge Focus on Coaching

The Focus on Coaching series features books which cover an aspect of coaching particularly dear to the author's or editor's heart that they wish to share with the wider professional coaching community. The series editors are Windy Dryden and David A. Lane.

For a full list of titles in this series, please visit www.routledge.com/Routledge-Focus-on-Coaching/book-series/RFC

Titles in the series

The Coaching Alliance
Theory and Guidelines for Practice
Windy Dryden

A Practical Guide to Rational Emotive Behavioural Coaching
Windy Dryden

A Practical Guide to Rational Emotive Behavioural Coaching

Windy Dryden

Routledge
Taylor & Francis Group
LONDON AND NEW YORK

First published 2018
by Routledge
2 Park Square, Milton Park, Abingdon, Oxon OX14 4RN

and by Routledge
711 Third Avenue, New York, NY 10017

Routledge is an imprint of the Taylor & Francis Group, an informa business

© 2018 Windy Dryden

The right of Windy Dryden to be identified as author of this work has been asserted by him in accordance with sections 77 and 78 of the Copyright, Designs and Patents Act 1988.

All rights reserved. No part of this book may be reprinted or reproduced or utilised in any form or by any electronic, mechanical, or other means, now known or hereafter invented, including photocopying and recording, or in any information storage or retrieval system, without permission in writing from the publishers.

Trademark notice: Product or corporate names may be trademarks or registered trademarks, and are used only for identification and explanation without intent to infringe.

British Library Cataloguing in Publication Data
A catalogue record for this book is available from the British Library

Library of Congress Cataloging in Publication Data
A catalog record for this book has been requested

ISBN: 978-0-815-34872-6 (hbk)
ISBN: 978-1-351-16608-9 (ebk)

Typeset in Times New Roman
by Out of House Publishing

Contents

	Introduction	1
1	Laying the foundations (LTF): Helping coachees to get the most from REBC	2
2	A step-based framework for the practice of emotional problem-focused REBC (EPF-REBC)	9
3	A step-based framework for the practice of practical problem-focused REBC (PPF-REBC)	32
4	A step-based framework for the practice of development-focused REBC (DF-REBC)	43
5	Ending REBC, follow-up and evaluation (EFE)	54
	Appendix 1: 20 healthy principles of living and development-focused coaching	*60*
	Notes	*66*
	References	*69*
	Index	*71*

Portions of this book appeared in a chapter entitled 'Rational-emotive, cognitive-behavior coaching: A step-based framework for practice' published in M.E. Bernard & O. David (Eds.) (2018), *Coaching Reason, Emotion and Behavioral Change: Rational-Emotive, Cognitive-Behavioral Practices.* New York: Springer. Reproduced with kind permission of the publisher.

Introduction

Coaching was originated to help people who are functioning satisfactorily in life to develop themselves in one or more life areas (Wildflower, 2013). I refer to this as development-focused coaching. However, coaches are also asked to help people deal with a range of practical and emotional problems because these people find it more acceptable to be 'in coaching' than 'in therapy or counselling'. I refer to this as problem-focused coaching. Even if coaches decide to be 'purists' and only see people for development-focused coaching, these people will experience obstacles (both practical and emotional) to the pursuit of their development-focused objectives[1] and will expect their coaches to help them address these obstacles. Therefore, coaches need to develop a range of skills to deal with a range of situations.

This book is based on the above assumption and will outline the steps and strategies that coaches using Rational Emotive Behavioural Coaching (REBC) should[2] employ as a guide when working with coachees in development-focused REBC and problem-focused REBC. Within problem-focused REBC, I will cover coaching for practical problems and coaching for emotional problems (including their emotional problems about their practical problems). I will also show how REB coaches can address the inevitable obstacles to coaching progress that are likely to occur in all types of REBC. I will outline the most common steps for each type of coaching and discuss common strategies for the implementation of each step. It is important to mention at the outset that this schema is intended to be a guide for the flexible practice of REBC. It is not intended that coaches should rigidly adhere to the framework presented.

1 Laying the foundations (LTF): Helping coachees to get the most from REBC

In this chapter, I will discuss how REB coaches lay the foundations so that their coachees can get the most from the process of REBC.

LTF: Step 1. Respond to an initial enquiry

When a person first contacts an REB coach, that person may be in the role of 'enquirer' (i.e. making enquiries about coaching) or in the role of 'applicant' (i.e. seeking help from the coach having decided to seek coaching help from that person). However, they should not yet be seen to occupy the role of 'coachee' until they and the coach have contracted to work with one another. Whatever is the case, the person requires a response to their initial enquiry.

LTF: Step 1. Strategy 1. Conduct a brief, real-time conversation

Whether the coach has responded themself to the person's initial enquiry, I suggest that they themself carry out a brief, real-time (e.g. telephone or Skype) conversation with the person, unless there is a good reason not to do so. In my experience, ten minutes should suffice for this conversation, the purpose of which is for the coach to give information to the person in the enquirer role and to ascertain what help the person in the applicant role is seeking. If it seems that there is compatibility between what the applicant seeks and what the coach can offer, the latter should invite the former to a face-to-face[1] assessment-based session, the purpose of which is to agree the type of coaching that is best suited to the person and to agree a coaching contract.[2]

LTF: Step 2. Ask the applicant to prepare for the face-to-face assessment session

One of the points that coaches can make at the outset is that they expect coachees to be active between coaching sessions. Thus, the REB coach can ask the applicant to prepare for the face-to-face assessment session.

LTF: Step 2. Strategy 1. Use a pre-assessment coaching questionnaire

Table 1 provides an example of a form the coach might suggest that the applicant completes before the session as one way of preparing for the session. Note that all the information requested is designed to provide the coach with information that will help the person get the most out of coaching, if they become a coachee.

Table 1: Pre-assessment coaching questionnaire

Please answer the following questions as honestly as you can. The information that you provide will help you get the most from coaching and help the coach tailor coaching to your individual situation. All information is confidential.

1. What do you hope to achieve from coaching?
2. What strengths do you have as a person that you can use during coaching that would help you get the most out of this process?
3. What resources in your environment do you have access to that could help you during the coaching process?
4. Which people in your life can you call upon to support and encourage you during coaching?

(*continued*)

Table 1: (Cont.)

5. What does your coach need to know about your learning style to help ensure that you get the most out of coaching?
6. What style of coaching should your coach ideally adopt to help you get the most out of coaching?
7. What are some of your core life values that your coach should know about?
8. What do you find meaningful in your life?
9. How much time are you prepared to devote to coaching-related activities per day?
10. Is there anything that you would like your coach to know or think your coach needs to know before coaching begins?

LTF: Step 3. Carry out a face-to-face assessment session

As noted above, a major purpose of the face-to-face assessment session is to help both the applicant and the REB coach determine whether coaching is the right form of help for the person and, if so, which type of REBC is best suited to the person.

LTF: Step 3. Strategy 1. *Determine which type of coaching the person is suitable for*

When working with the applicant to see if the person is suitable for REBC and if so, which type, the following criteria can be used:

For development-focused coaching. Here, the applicant is doing satisfactorily in life and wishes to develop themself in one or more areas of their life. During the recent past, the person has neither experienced an emotional problem nor a practical problem that required professional help.

For emotional problem-focused coaching. Here, the applicant has an emotional problem or problems where the person has emotionally disturbed reactions to one or more adversities. The question arises as to whether the person should see an REB coach or an REB therapist. Cavanagh (2005) suggests that coaching is suitable for emotional problems when:

1. The emotional problem is of recent origin or occurs intermittently.
2. The responses of the person to the main adversity are distressing to the person, but lie within a mild to moderate range of distress.
3. The person's emotional problem is limited to a certain situation or aspect of the person's life.
4. The person is not defensive with respect to the problem.
5. The person is open to addressing and changing the problem.

To these, I would add that the person wants to see a coach and would not consult a therapist or counsellor, for example, because of the stigma of doing so.

For practical problem-focused coaching. Here, the applicant is confused, tangled up with an issue or issues and needs clarity and order, which they hope to get by talking things through with someone, but they are not emotionally disturbed about the issue(s). If they do have an emotional problem about their practical problem, the former in REBC is generally tackled before the latter, as the presence of the emotional problem will impede and distract the person from focusing on solving the practical problem.

LTF: Step 3. Strategy 2. Determine if the person is suitable for REBC

Once the coach and applicant have decided which type of coaching is suitable for the person, then the coach should literally give an overview of the REB approach to coaching so that they can both determine whether this type of coaching is suitable for the person and is what the person is looking for. While each coach will tailor this overview for each applicant, the following is an indication about what should be covered in the overview:

Development-focused REBC. Here, the coach should say that the focus will be on enhancing the person's development and that this process can be underpinned by REBC's rational principles of living that have been outlined in Bernard (2018a). Examples of such principles should be given to the coachee so they know what the coach means. It is important that the coach explains that while it would be good if the person makes unimpeded progress towards their development-based objectives, obstacles to that progress may well arise and, if so, the coach will help the person address these obstacles by examining the thinking, emotion and behaviour implicated in the obstacles and changing those aspects, which will result in the resumption of objective-focused coaching.

Emotional problem-focused REBC. Here, the coach should say that addressing the person's emotional problems will be done by setting goals and then helping them to identify and change the rigid and extreme attitudes that underpin their problems. Goals are achieved by attitude change, which occurs when the person acts in ways that are consistent with their alternative flexible and non-extreme attitudes while facing problem-related adversities. Again, the coach should explain that while it would be good if the person makes unimpeded progress towards their problem-based goals, obstacles to that progress may well arise and, if so, the coach will help the person address these obstacles by using similar methods that are employed in helping them address their emotional problems. Once this is done, resumption of problem-focused coaching can occur.

Practical problem-focused REBC. Here, the coach should say that addressing the person's practical problem will be done by helping them to learn and apply a practical problem-solving framework designed to help them identify and evaluate a range of possible solutions and to apply the one most likely to be successful. In addition, the coach should say that if the person has an emotional problem about their practical problem, then this

Laying the foundations 7

former problem needs to be tackled before the latter and, if so, the coach's explanation should be as in the previous section. Similar points about obstacles to progress in practical problem-focused REBC should be made as were made in the other two types of REBC detailed above.

Once the person and the coach have jointly decided that REBC is a suitable approach, have selected the type of REBC to be used, have discussed issues arising from the person's responses to the pre-assessment questionnaire presented in Table 1 and have settled a number of practical issues, then a coaching contract should be agreed and signed, if this is the coach's practice. At this point, the applicant becomes a coachee.

LTF: Step 3. Strategy 3. Decide with the coachee how you are both going to evaluate coaching

REBC is an evidence-based approach to coaching (see David, David & Razvan, 2018) and therefore the coach is concerned with evaluating their work with all coachees. At this point, I suggest that the REB coach ask the coachee how best they think that they both can evaluate their work. If the person defers to the coach on this question (as frequently happens), the coach should suggest that the two of them evaluate coaching outcomes and progress with respect to: (a) whichever problem the coachee seeks help for in problem-focused REBC and the goal related to the problem; and (b) whichever objective is chosen in development-focused REBC. Once this has been agreed, the coach may suggest how this may be done. I will revisit this latter issue later in this book in the 'EPF: Step 3' section.

LTF: Step 3. Strategy 4. Help the coachee to identify and use their strengths in REBC

Coachees bring to REBC a range of strengths that can help them get the most out of all three types of REBC to be discussed in this book. Thus, it is important for the coach to help the coachee identify these strengths and specify how these might be used in coaching.

Strengths are the internal attributes or personality traits and characteristics that can help the coachee get the most out of REBC. They can be assessed by the coach asking several questions. For example:

- "What would you say are your strengths as a person that you can bring to the coaching process?"

- "What would others who know you well say were your strengths as a person that you can bring to the coaching process?"
- "If you were being interviewed for a job and you were asked what strengths you had as a person, how would you respond?"

Once identified and noted, the coach can then encourage the coachee to use these strengths at salient points in the coaching process.

LTF: Step 3. Strategy 5. Help your coachee to identify and use their resources in REBC

If strengths are "the internal attributes or personality traits and characteristics that can help the coachee in REBC" (see above), resources are the practical tools or people present in the coachee's life that are available to assist in coaching. The example I often use when helping a coachee to distinguish between a strength and a resource is this: if a person wants to hire someone to help them to move house, they will look for someone who is dependable (strength) and who has a reliable van (resource). One without the other will be less effective than both together.

Here are some sample questions the coach can ask their coachee about their resources:

- "What resources do you have access to that could help you during coaching? If you don't have access to these resources, is there anybody who can help you get access to them?"
- "Which people do you have access to who may help you during coaching? Who are they and what can each of them bring to the situation that may be helpful to you in coaching?"
- "What information do you need that will help you during coaching? Where can you get this information?"
- "What resources in the community might be helpful to you during coaching?"

Once again, when these resources are identified and noted, the coach can then encourage the coachee to use them at salient points in the coaching process.

2 A step-based framework for the practice of emotional problem-focused REBC (EPF-REBC)[1]

In this section, I will deal with the steps that the REB coach is called upon to make when: (a) their coachee is seeking help for an emotional problem (EP) or problems; and (b) the coachee, in any type of REBC, experiences emotionally based obstacles[2] to coaching progress. Examples of common problems people bring to coaching are anxiety, unhealthy anger, guilt, shame and hurt.

EPF-REBC: Step 1. Select a Target Emotional Problem (TEP)

The REB coach prefers to work with one EP at a time, particularly at the beginning of coaching, and if the coachee has more than one problem, they both need to decide which problem they are going to focus on first. This is known as the TEP.

[In this book, I will use an example where Sarah sought coaching for problems with guilt.[3]]

EPF-REBC: Step 1. Strategy 1. Ask for the EP directly

REBC is an active-directive approach to coaching and in EPF-REBC this means asking the coachee directly for which problem or problems they are seeking help. "What problem can I help you with?" is a typical question that an REB coach would ask their coachee.

Framework for the practice of EPF-REBC

EPF-REBC: Step 1. Strategy 2. Work with the coachee to select the TEP

If the coachee only has one EP for which they are seeking coaching, then that automatically becomes the TEP.

[This was the case with Sarah.]

However, if they have more than one EP, then the coach needs to help them to select the TEP. This might be according to the coachee's choice, the easiest problem to tackle, the most serious problem or the problem that, if dealt with, would give the coachee hope that the other problems could be tackled. Unless the coach has a rationale for the selection of the TEP, in which case this should be shared with the coachee, the coach should go along with the coachee here. However, once selected, coach and coachee should ideally stick with the TEP unless there is a good reason to change focus.

EPF-REBC: Step 2. Assess the TEP

Once the TEP has been selected, it needs to be assessed. In REBC, the coach uses the 'Situational ABC-G' part of the 'Situational ABCDEFG' framework. The full framework is presented in Figure 1. Reference will be made to different parts of this framework throughout this book.

EPF-REBC: Step 2. Strategy 1. Use a specific example of the TEP

Perhaps the best way of assessing the TEP in REBC is for the coach and coachee to work with a specific example of this problem. Specificity encourages the eliciting of information that is likely to be emotionally salient and allow a more valid assessment of the TEP. The specific example might be recent, typical, vivid or anticipated. The coach should work with the coachee to select an example that best aids the assessment process.

EPF-REBC: Step 3. Assessment of TEP: Help the coachee to describe the 'situation'

The first step in the assessment process is for the coach to help the coachee to describe the situation in which the example of the EP occurred: where

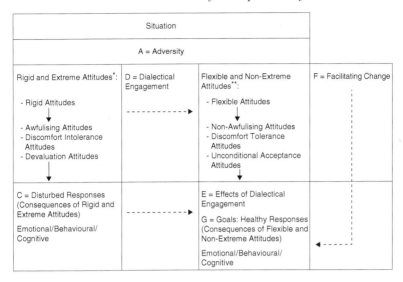

Figure 1: Situational ABCDEFG framework
* In REBC theory, a rigid attitude is regarded as the primary attitude underpinning psychological disturbance, with the extreme attitudes as listed derived from it
** In REBC theory, a flexible attitude is regarded as the primary attitude underpinning psychological health, with the non-extreme attitudes as listed derived from it

did it take place, who was present and what factually was said and done by those present. Help the coachee distinguish between a situation (what happened) and an inference (their interpretation of what happened). The latter will be assessed shortly (see step 5 below).

[Sarah selected an example where she wanted to go out with her friends but didn't because she would have felt guilty about leaving her mother on her own.]

EPF-REBC: Step 4. Assessment of TEP: Identify 'C'

The coachee is seeking help for an EP largely because they are experiencing an unhealthy negative emotion[4] (UNE). It is important that the coach asks the person to identify this emotion. This is likely to be one of the following: anxiety, depression, guilt, shame, problematic anger, hurt, problematic jealousy or problematic envy.

EPF-REBC: Step 4. Strategy 1. Help the coachee select their main UNE

It may be that the person mentions more than one UNE when the coach asks them for their main emotion in the chosen situation. As each emotion may be about a different facet of the situation, it is important that the coach helps the coachee to select one emotion to target for change at a time and preferably the emotion that best reflects the problem for which they are seeking help.

[Sarah's UNE was guilt.]

EPF-REBC: Step 4. Strategy 2. Clarify a vague UNE

It may be that the coachee says that they feel "bad" or "upset" in response to a question about 'C'. If this happens, it is important that the coach helps the coachee to clarify what they mean, as it is more difficult to work with a poorly understood emotion in REBC than a clearly understood one. One way of doing this is to show the coachee the list of UNEs provided above and ask which best describes their "bad" or "upset" feeling.

EPF-REBC: Step 4. Strategy 3. Respond when the coachee confuses an emotion with an inference

Sometimes a coachee will offer an inference as an emotion when asked how they felt in the described situation.

[Initially when asked about her feeling at 'C', Sarah said, "I felt selfish."]

When this happens, explain the difference between the two and then ask how they felt about the inference.

["Selfish is a behaviour not an emotion. How did you feel about acting selfishly?" Sarah responded that she felt guilt.]

EPF-REBC: Step 4. Strategy 4. Identify the behavioural 'C'

When you have clearly identified the coachee's UNE, you can then help them to identify the actual behaviours or action tendencies that accompanied the UNE in the problem example (e.g. "When you felt hurt, what did you do ... and what did you feel like doing, but decided not to do?").

[In response to this question, Sarah said that she decided not to go out with her friends.]

These behavioural factors are likely to be unconstructive for the person and tend to maintain the EP.

EPF-REBC: Step 4. Strategy 5. Identify the cognitive 'C', if necessary

When the coachee experiences a UNE, they also have a tendency to think in certain ways. These tend to be highly distorted, skewed to the negative and ruminative in nature because they are the cognitive consequences of holding rigid and extreme attitudes (REAs) about adversities. When assessing these cognitive 'C's, the coach asks such questions as: "Once you felt 'x', what thoughts accompanied this feeling?" and "Were you easily able to let go of these thoughts or were you ruminating on them?"

[In response to these questions, Sarah responded that she thought, "Something very bad will happen to my mother if I leave her," and that she did ruminate on this thought.]

EPF-REBC: Step 5. Assessment of TEP: Identify 'A'

Once the coach has assessed the coachee's emotive, behavioural and cognitive 'C's in the problem example, they can now take the emotive part and use it to identify the person's 'A', which is the aspect of the situation about which the coachee is most disturbed or finds most problematic. There are many ways of assessing 'A' (see Dryden & Branch, 2008). I will present one that I particularly employ in coaching.

EPF-REBC: Step 5. Strategy 1. An example of assessing 'A'

Table 2 outlines how to use a technique called 'Windy's Magic Question' to identify 'A'.

14 Framework for the practice of EPF-REBC

Table 2: Windy's Magic Question

> **Purpose**: To help the coachee to identify the 'A' in the 'Situational ABC-G' framework as quickly as possible (i.e. what the coachee is most disturbed about) once 'C' has been assessed and the situation in which 'C' has occurred has been identified and briefly described.
>
> **Point 1**: Have the coachee focus on their disturbed 'C' (in our example, 'guilt').
>
> **Point 2**: Have the coachee focus on the situation in which 'C' occurred (e.g. "My friends were going out and I decided not to go out with them because it meant leaving my mother on her own").
>
> **Point 3**: Ask the coachee, "Which ingredient could we give you to eliminate or significantly reduce 'C'?" (in our example, 'guilt'; in this case, the coachee said, "not acting selfishly"). Take care that the coachee does not change the situation (that Sarah does not say, "my friends not going out").
>
> **Point 4**: The opposite is probably "A" (e.g. "acting selfishly"), but check this. Ask, "So when you were thinking of going out, were you most guilty about acting selfishly if you decided to go out and leave your mother alone?" If not, use the question in Point 3 again until the coachee confirms what they were most guilty about in the described situation.

EPF-REBC: Step 5. Strategy 2. Encourage the coachee to assume temporarily that 'A' is true

REBC theory holds that the best way to help a coachee with their TEP is to encourage them to face the adversity that they find problematic and thence to develop flexible and non-extreme attitudes (FNAs) about this adversity. To do this, the coach suggests that they assume temporarily that 'A' is true rather than questioning whether it was the most probable interpretation what happened.

> *[In our example, this meant that Sarah assumed that she would be acting selfishly if she decided to go out and leave her mother alone even if there was a more accurate interpretation of her behaviour.]*

There will be a later opportunity for the coachee to question 'A'.

EPF-REBC: Step 6. Assessment of TEP: Elicit 'G'

Coaching works best when the coachee sets a goal and the coach helps them to achieve it (Gessnitzer & Kauffeld, 2015). At this point of the process, the coachee needs to discover what this goal is.

EPF-REBC: Step 6. Strategy 1. Ask for goals in relation to 'A'

However, care needs to be taken here and the coach needs to help the coachee understand that in order to deal effectively with their problem, they need to develop more constructive responses at 'G' to *each* of the problematic emotional, behavioural and cognitive responses (i.e. 'C's) to the adversity at 'A'. These constructive responses become the coachee's goals. Thus, the coach should ask such questions as:

[*"If you did act selfishly in this situation, what would be a healthy way of responding to this emotionally, behaviourally and thinking-wise?" "What could you feel instead of 'guilt'?" "What could you do instead of not going out with your friends and what could you think instead of concluding that something very bad will happen to your mother if I do leave her?"*]

EPF-REBC: Step 6. Strategy 2. Elicit a healthy negative emotion (HNE) in response to a UNE

In response to being asked for a constructive emotional goal with respect to 'A', the coachee may give a positive or a neutral emotional goal. For example:

[*"I don't want to feel bothered about going out with my friends."*]

The coach needs to help the coachee see that given the fact that it is important for her not to act selfishly (assuming again that she is acting in a selfish manner), for example, acting selfishly is an adversity or a negative event and it is not realistic or healthy to strive to feel good or neutral about something bad. I often help my coachees understand that their choice is to feel bad with disturbance (i.e. UNE) or bad without disturbance (i.e. HNE).[5]

[Sarah's coach helped her to see that feeling remorse, but not guilt, was a healthy emotional response to acting selfishly and was associated with more constructive behaviour (going out with her friends) and balanced thinking (concluding that while something very bad might happen to her mother when she was out, this was quite unlikely).]

EPF-REBC: Step 7. Assessment of TEP: Make the general 'B–C' connection

The 'ABC' part of the 'Situational ABCDEFG' framework is perhaps the heart of the REBC model. While this part emphasises that it is the basic attitudes that people hold towards adversities that largely determine how they respond to it, at this point of the process, the REB coach is content to help their coachee see that their responses are largely determined by how they think about adversities and not by the adversities themselves.

EPF-REBC: Step 8. Assessment of TEP: Identify rigid and extreme attitudes (REAs) and flexible and non-extreme attitudes (FNAs) and connect to 'C' and 'G'

Some REB coaches prefer to incorporate step 7 into step 8. Here, the coach helps the person to identify the REAs that underpin their problematic responses ('C') to the adversity at 'A' and also the FNAs that underpin their constructive responses ('G') to the same adversity.

EPF-REBC: Step 8. Strategy 1. An example of identifying REA/FNA and connecting REA/C and FNA/G

Table 3 outlines how to use a technique called 'Windy's Review Assessment Procedure' (WRAP) to identify simultaneously a coachee's REA and FNA and connecting these to 'C' and 'G', respectively. The content in this table is taken from the work done by Sarah and her coach.

EPF-REBC: Step 8. Strategy 2. Work with the primary rigid attitude and flexible attitude and one of the derivatives from these respective attitudes

In Table 3, I demonstrated the WRAP method of identifying and connecting the rigid attitude with its consequences and the flexible attitude with its consequences. In REBC theory, a rigid attitude is seen as the primary unconstructive attitude, with awfulising, discomfort intolerance

Table 3: Windy's Review Assessment Procedure (WRAP)

Purpose: Once 'C' (e.g. 'guilt') and 'A' (e.g. 'acting selfishly') have been assessed, this technique can be used to identify both the coachee's rigid and extreme attitudes ('REAs') and their alterative flexible and non-extreme attitudes ('FNAs') and to help the coachee to understand the connection between their 'REAs' and 'C' and their 'FNAs' and their goals at 'G'. This technique can be used with the coachee's rigid attitude versus flexible attitude (as shown below) and with any of the derivative extreme and non-extreme attitudes from this pairing (see Figure 1).

Step 1: Say, "Let's review what we know and what we don't know so far."

Step 2: Say, "We know three things. First, we know that you felt guilt ('C'). Second, we know that you felt guilt about acting selfishly ('A'). Third, and this is an educated guess on my part, we know that it is important to you not to act selfishly. Am I correct?"

Assuming that the coachee confirms the coach's hunch, note that what the coach has done is to identify the part of the attitude that is common to both the coachee's rigid attitude and alternative flexible attitude, as we will see.

Step 3: Say, "Now let's review what we don't know. This is where I need your help. We don't know which of the two attitudes your guilt was based on. So, when you felt guilty about acting selfishly, was your guilt based on Attitude 1: 'It is important to me that I don't act selfishly and therefore I must not do so' ('rigid attitude') or Attitude 2: 'It is important to me that I don't selfishly, but unfortunately that does not mean that I must not do so' ('flexible attitude')?"

Step 4: If necessary, help the coachee to understand that their 'C' (guilt) was based on their rigid attitude if they are unsure.

Step 5: Once the coachee is clear that their guilt was based on their rigid attitude, make and emphasise the rigid attitude-disturbed 'C' connection. Then ask, "Now, let's suppose instead that you had a strong conviction in Attitude 2, how would you feel about acting selfishly if you strongly held the attitude that while it was important to you not to act selfishly, unfortunately that does not mean that you must not do so?"

(continued)

18 *Framework for the practice of EPF-REBC*

Table 3: (*Cont.*)

Step 6: If necessary, remind the coachee of the emotional goal (healthy negative emotion) that you negotiated with them as per the 'EPF-REBC: Step 6. Strategy 2' section (i.e. remorse), if not immediately volunteered, and make and emphasise the flexible attitude–G connection.
Step 7: Ensure the coachee clearly understands the differences between the rigid attitude–C and flexible attitude–G connections.
Step 8: Reinforce the healthy negative emotion that the coachee has set as their emotional goal (i.e. remorse) and encourage them to see that developing conviction in their flexible attitude is the best way of achieving this goal.

and devaluation attitudes seen as extreme derivatives from this primary attitude (see Figure 1). Similarly, a flexible attitude is seen as the primary constructive attitude, with non-awfulising, discomfort tolerance and acceptance attitudes seen as non-extreme derivatives from this primary attitude (see Figure 1). With respect to assessment, I suggest that the coach help the coachee to identify the one main derivative of these two primary attitudes and connect these with their consequences.

EPF-REBC: Step 9. Prepare for dialectical engagement[6]

The coachee now understands the relationship between their REAs and their consequences at 'C' and between their FNAs and their goals at 'G'. Before helping the coachee to examine their attitudes (a process that I call 'dialectical engagement'), the coach needs to prepare the coachee for this process, otherwise the coachee may not understand why the coach is asking them questions. Saying something like the following should suffice: "I am going to ask you some questions so you can think about both sets of attitudes that we have been discussing and can commit to one set and know why you are committing to it. Is this OK with you?"

EPF-REBC: Step 10. Dialectical engagement

As shown above, engaging the coachee in a dialectical examination of their attitudes involves the coach asking the coachee questions of both sets of attitudes: rigid and extreme and flexible and non-extreme. In doing so, the following points should be borne in mind.

EPF-REBC: Step 10. Strategy 1. Help the coachee to see the purpose of dialectical engagement

Dialectical engagement has a purpose and it is to help the coachee see that their REAs are false, illogical and largely have unhealthy consequences and their FNAs are true, logical and largely have healthy consequences. Ellis (1963) has called this 'intellectual insight' and while it is insufficient on its own to facilitate therapeutic change, it is very important as it helps the person see why they should let go of their REAs and develop conviction in their FNAs. In the 'Situational ABCDEFG' framework, this represents 'E' or the effects of dialectical engagement.

EPF-REBC: Step 10. Strategy 2. Use order in dialectical engagement

While there is no set order in which REAs and FNAs are to be examined, one of the most efficient ways of questioning attitudes is to take one of the coachee's REAs and alternative FNAs and question them both at the same time (see below) (e.g. "Which of these two attitudes is true and which is false and why?").

EPF-REBC: Step 10. Strategy 3. Use three standpoints in dialectical engagement

DiGiuseppe (1991) cogently argued that there are three standpoints from where REAs and FNAs can be examined[7]: (i) empirical ("Which of these attitudes is true and which is false and why?"); (ii) logical ("Which of these two attitudes is logical and which is illogical and why?") and (iii) pragmatic ("Which of these two attitudes is helpful and which is unhelpful to you and why?"). While a coachee may find a particular standpoint convincing, the coach only discovers this by using all three in dialectical engagement.

[Sarah's coach suggested that she consider both her rigid attitude and her flexible attitude at the same time and asked her which of the two was true and which false, which logical and which illogical and which yielded good results and which yielded poor results. Sarah's coach asked her to give reasons for her answers.]

EPF-REBC: Step 10. Strategy 4. Use a variety of styles in dialectical engagement

DiGiuseppe (1991) also outlined a variety of styles that the REB coach can use in examining attitudes with the coachee. It is important that the coach becomes adept at using these styles at different junctures and with different coachees, but to do so authentically (Lazarus, 1993). Such styles include:

- *Socratic*, where the coach asks the coachee a series of guided questions designed to help the coachee to discover the answers for themself.
- *Didactic*, where the coach teaches a salient point that will clarify matters for the coachee. Here, it is important that the coach ensures that the coachee has understood the point made by asking them to put the point into their own words.
- *Metaphorical*, where the coach uses a story, parable, aphorism or saying to make a point. Again, checking for coachee understanding of the point is important.
- *Self-disclosing*, where the coach makes a point by sharing a relevant experience from their own life. Coping self-disclosure (where a coach says that they used to experience a similar problem to the coachee but addressed it by using similar insights that they wish the coachee to consider) is more persuasive than mastery self-disclosure (where the coach states that have used these insights to prevent the development of the problem). It is important for the coach to ask for coachee permission to use self-disclosure as not all coachees find coach self-disclosure useful and/or appropriate. Eliciting coachee feedback after the disclosure is also important, even when such permission has been granted.
- *Humorous*, where the coach uses humour to encourage the coachee to see the funny side of an REA with the intent of helping them to change it. Here, the coach needs to guard against using humour that could be experienced as 'ad hominem' by the coachee. In this respect, seeking coachee feedback is crucial.

EPF-REBC: Step 10. Strategy 5. Use persuasive arguments

While there are guidelines to follow when examining attitudes with the coachee, it is important for the coach to recognise that what one coachee finds persuasive another won't. The coach needs to use their creative intuition in making dialectical engagement interventions based on their knowledge of the coachee in question and their experience of working with the person. Having said that, in my experience, there are a few arguments that are routinely persuasive. One is what I call 'teach your children well'.[8] Here, I take the coachee's rigid and flexible attitude pairing, for example, and ask them which attitude they would teach their children, which they would not and the reason for their choice. I then ask them what would stop them from doing the same for themselves. The resultant discussion often reveals the person's doubts, reservations and objections to letting go of REAs and developing FNAs.

[Sarah found the 'teach your children well' technique particularly powerful and recognised that as there was no special reason why she would hold on to her rigid attitude while encouraging any children that she might have in the future to let such an attitude go. This provided the commitment she needed to develop her flexible attitude and to let her rigid attitude go.]

EPF-REBC: Step 11. Deal with the coachee's doubts, reservations and objections (DROs)

As I mentioned above, a coachee may have DROs to letting go of their REAs and developing their alternative FNAs. The coachee may disclose these DROs or they may hold them implicitly and not disclose them. Given this, it is useful for the REB coach to ask their coachee routinely if they have such DROs and, if so, to help them to see that they are usually based on a misconception.

[Thus, Sarah revealed that she was reluctant to let go of her rigid attitude that she must not act selfishly because she thought that doing so meant that she was condoning such behaviour. Her coach helped her to see that neither her rigid attitude nor her alternative flexible attitude condoned bad behaviour. Rather, these attitudes were concerned with whether she must not act selfishly or whether such a rigid demand does not exist even though her preference does.]

EPF-REBC: Step 12. Prepare the coachee to deepen conviction in their FNAs

As I said earlier, the purpose of dialectical engagement is to help the coachee understand intellectually that their REAs are false, illogical and yield poor results and their alternative FNAs are true, logical and yield good results and the reasons why this is ('E' in the 'Situational ABCDEFG' framework). Once this has been done, the coach needs to help the coachee develop emotional insight into these ideas, which means, in effect, that their conviction in their FNAs is deepened to the point that these attitudes have a constructive impact on the emotional, behavioural and cognitive responses to the adversity at 'A'. This represents 'F' in the 'Situational ABCDEFG' framework, which stands for 'facilitating change'. For this to be done, the coachee needs to rehearse these FNAs while acting in ways that are consistent with them when facing examples of the adversity. Before the coach helps the coachee to do this, they need to help the person understand and commit to this change process. This should be done at this point of the process.

EPF-REBC: Step 13. Negotiate homework tasks

The main way that a coachee can develop greater conviction in their FNAs during REBC is by carrying out agreed homework tasks between sessions.

EPF-REBC: Step 13. Strategy 1. Negotiate tasks, don't assign them unilaterally

I prefer the term 'task' to the term 'assignment' when discussing what a coachee is going to do for homework because the term 'assignment' means something is assigned to the coachee to do, while the term 'task' does not have this connotation. Thus, the REB coach negotiates a task with the coachee and does not assign to the person. The more the coachee is involved in the construction of the task, the more likely it is that they will do it (Kazantzis, Whittington & Dattilio, 2010).

EPF-REBC: Step 13. Strategy 2. Take time to negotiate a task

Homework tasks are usually negotiated at the end of the coaching session. Enough time needs to be devoted to the negotiation process if the selected task is likely to be done and add value to the process.

EPF-REBC: Step 13. Strategy 3. Ensure that the task is related to the work done in the coaching session

A good homework task follows logically from what is discussed in a coaching session rather than being unrelated or peripherally related to the session focus.

Framework for the practice of EPF-REBC 23

EPF-REBC: Step 13. Strategy 4. Help the coachee to see the purpose of the agreed task

The purpose of an effective homework task is to provide the coachee with the opportunity to face a relevant adversity while rehearsing the person's FNAs without the use of safety-seeking procedures (both behavioural and cognitive) designed to help the person avoid the adversity or keep themselves safe if they cannot avoid it. The main problem with these procedures, which are often subtle in nature, is that they prevent the coachee from fully facing the adversity and processing it in healthy ways. Consequently, it is important for the coach to help the coachee identify their routinely used safety-seeking procedures and to encourage them to drop their use while carrying out homework tasks.

EPF-REBC: Step 13. Strategy 5. Ensure that the coachee has the skills or capability to do the task

If the coachee does not have the skills to carry out a homework task and they can be taught these skills by the coach quite easily, then the coach should do this and then negotiate the task. However, if the skill is more complex and will take a while to be taught and acquired or the coachee lacks the capability to carry out the task, then another task should be considered.

EPF-REBC: Step 13. Strategy 6. Encourage the coachee to face the adversity whenever possible and to use the 'challenging, but not overwhelming' principle while doing so (Dryden, 1985)

This states that the coachee should face an adversity when it is challenging to do so, but not if is overwhelming for the coachee to do so. If the task is too easy, then it has little therapeutic value, but if it is too tough, then the person will not do it and may become discouraged with coaching.

EPF-REBC: Step 13. Strategy 7. Attend to the specifics when negotiating a task

An effective homework task is one where the person carries out a specific task on a specific number of occasions in specific situations at specific times. Consequently, the coach should encourage the coachee to use the concept of specificity while negotiating homework tasks.

24 Framework for the practice of EPF-REBC

EPF-REBC: Step 13. Strategy 8. Suggest that the coachee makes a written note of the negotiated homework task

Rather than commit the negotiated task to memory, the coachee is more likely to remember it if they make a written note of it in a place to which they have ready access (e.g. a frequently consulted diary, in a notebook or on a smartphone).

EPF-REBC: Step 13. Strategy 9. Problem-solve any obstacles to task completion

With homework negotiation, it is better to be forewarned than forearmed. Consequently, the coach should ask the coachee to identify potential obstacles to task completion and find ways of dealing with these to prevent them from becoming actual obstacles.

EPF-REBC: Step 13. Strategy 10. Suggest that the coachee uses imagery rehearsal in the session and between sessions

Before carrying out the task 'in the field', as it were, the coach can suggest that the coachee pictures themself facing the adversity, acting constructively and holding in mind the FNAs that they wish to develop. This can be done first in the coaching session and later outside the session, but before the coachee carries out the task in reality.

[Sarah agreed to carry out tasks that helped her to rehearse her FNAs towards acting selfishly. Thus, she decided that even if it were selfish to leave her mother alone once a week, she was going to put herself first at times and that there was no law that decreed that she must not act selfishly, if indeed it was selfish to leave her mother once a week to do so. She reminded herself that she was a fallible human being with many good and bad points and that she was not a bad and selfish person for acting selfishly. Sarah was tempted to agree with her friends that she wasn't acting selfishly under these circumstances, but her coach encouraged her to hold to the 'let's assume you are acting selfishly' strategy in order to give her the opportunity to change her attitude about her assumed 'selfish behaviour'. Sarah practised this once a week over the course of coaching until she had developed real conviction in her FNA towards putting herself first and that this attitude effected for the better her emotions, behaviour and subsequent thinking.]

EPF-REBC: Step 14. Review homework tasks

Unless there is a good reason not to, it is important that the REB coach reviews the coachee's homework task at the beginning of the following session. Not reviewing this task communicates implicitly to the coachee that homework tasks are not important. When reviewing homework tasks with a coachee, it is important for the REB coach to use several important strategies.

EPF-REBC: Step 14. Strategy 1. Discover what the person actually did for homework

Ensure that the coachee did the task as agreed and explore and, if necessary, respond to any modifications that they made to the task.

EPF-REBC: Step 14. Strategy 2. Evaluate success by the coachee's efforts and behaviour on the task rather than its outcome

Thus, if a coachee agreed to assert themself with one person a day, then, if they did this, it was a success, no matter how the other people responded to them.

EPF-REBC: Step 14. Strategy 3. Respond to the coachee's failure to carry out the task

It is important that the coach assesses and responds to the coachee's failure to initiate or complete the task with understanding and not censure. This will encourage the coachee to be honest about the reasons for task non-completion.

EPF-REBC: Step 14. Strategy 4. Respond to the coachee's routine failure to carry out homework tasks

When a coachee routinely fails to do homework tasks, it is useful to use REBC's 'Situational ABCDEFG' framework to help them deal with any emotionally based obstacles to task completion.

EPF-REBC: Step 14. Strategy 5. Capitalise on the coachee's success

It is important that the coach helps the coachee to articulate what they learned from doing the task and capitalises on their success by helping them to generalise that learning.

[Sarah's coach said: "You successfully put yourself first and went out with your friends while rehearsing the attitude that, while it may be selfish to leave your mother alone, doing so proves that you are a fallible human being who may have been wrong in putting yourself first on that occasion. How could you apply this learning to other instances of your problems with guilt?"]

EPF-REBC: Step 15. Encourage the coachee to re-examine 'A'

You will recall that in the 'EPF-REBC: Step 5. Strategy 2' section, the coach encouraged the coachee to assume temporarily that 'A' was true, even if it was clearly distorted. This was to help both to work at the attitude level rather than the inference level. However, after the coachee has made some progress in developing their FNAs, they are ready, if necessary, to stand back and question 'A'.

EPF-REBC: Step 15. Strategy 1. Use the most commonly used way of re-examining 'A'

The most common approach to re-examining 'A' employed by REB coaches involves the coach encouraging the coachee to go back to the 'Situational ABCDEFG' assessment, focus on the 'situation' and then have them ask themself whether the inference that they made at 'A' was the most realistic way of viewing the situation given all the evidence to hand. This involves considering the inference made at 'A', considering alternative inferences, evaluating all the possibilities and choosing the most realistic inference.

[Sarah asked herself how likely it was that her wanting to go out with her friends while leaving her mother on her own was evidence of selfish behaviour. In answering this question, Sarah considered the possibility that her behaviour was not selfish as she spends six nights with her mother a week and that it was quite understandable that she would want to have time for herself. She concluded that, on reflection and free from the influence of guilt, her behaviour was not selfish. It is important to note the timing of this strategy: it is done after the coachee has had an opportunity to change her attitude towards her adversity. Free from the influence of her REAs towards acting selfishly, Sarah was able to be more objective about her inference that it was selfish to leave her mother once a week.]

EPF-REBC: Step 15. Strategy 2. Help the coachee use other ways of re-examining 'A'

These involve the coachee asking themself:

- How likely is it that 'A' happened (or might happen)?
- Would an objective jury agree that 'A' happened or might happen? If not, what would the jury's verdict be?
- Did I view (or am I viewing) the situation realistically? If not, how could I have viewed (or can I view) it more realistically?
- If I asked someone whom I could trust to give me an objective opinion about the truth or falsity of my inference about the situation at hand, what would the person say to me and why? How would this person encourage me to view the situation instead?
- If a friend had told me that they had faced (or were facing or were about to face) the same situation as I faced and had made the same inference, what would I say to him/her about the validity of their inference and why? How would I encourage the person to view the situation instead?

EPF-REBC: Step 16. Help the coachee to generalise their learning

The coach can help the coachee to generalise their learning in EPF-REBC in several ways.

EPF-REBC: Step 16. Strategy 1. Encourage generalisation across adversity-related situations

A common generalisation strategy is for the coach to ask the coachee to nominate other specific situations where they may encounter the adversity and then encourage the coachee to face up to those situations while practicing their developing FNAs.

[Using this strategy, Sarah's coach said: "What other situations are there where you think you would be acting selfishly and where you might face these situations while rehearing the idea that you are a fallible human being who is acting selfishly?" Sarah nominated several such situations and her coach helped her to make a plan to face these situations in a stepwise manner. Sarah did this and became more

28 Framework for the practice of EPF-REBC

adept at getting what she wanted out of life and less manipulated by others attempts to 'make her feel guilty'.]

EPF-REBC: Step 16. Strategy 2. Encourage generalisation across emotions

Alternatively, the coach can ask the coachee to practice their FNAs in situations where they would normally feel the UNE in their target problem.

EPF-REBC: Step 16. Strategy 3. Encourage belief-focused generalisation

Perhaps the most advanced strategy in generalisation enhancement involves the coach encouraging the coachee to take the general form of a specific FNA and to seek out situations where they can then practice it.

[Using this strategy, Sarah's coach would have said: "In what other contexts can you rehearse the belief that you are a fallible human being even if you act selfishly?" Then the coach would help Sarah to implement this, again in a stepwise fashion.]

EPF-REBC: Step 17. Identify, understand and deal with obstacles[9]

An obstacle in EPF-REBC is something that blocks the coachee's path towards their goal with respect to their EP. In this section, I will focus mainly on obstacles to which the coachee responds in an unhealthy way emotionally, behaviourally and cognitively. The aim here is to help the coachee deal with the obstacle so that they can return to the business of pursuing their coaching goal. Please note that what I have to say about identifying, understanding and dealing with actual obstacles can also be applied to helping the coachee anticipate, understand and deal with potential obstacles.

EPF-REBC: Step 17. Strategy 1. Identify the type of obstacle the coachee is facing and respond accordingly

There are four types of obstacle that the coachee might encounter:

- An external adversity occurs that is related to the REBC process (e.g. someone criticises the coachee as they put into practice their coaching plan).

Here, the coach can help the coachee address the obstacle using either the 'PRACTICE' problem-solving framework (discussed in Chapter 3 and summarised in Table 4) if the coachee's obstacle is indicative of a practical problem or the 'Situational ABCDEFG' framework if it is indicative of an emotional problem.

- An external adversity occurs that is not related to the REBC process (e.g. one of coachee's relatives is very ill).

If the coachee has an EP about this, then the coach can help by using the 'Situational ABCDEFG' framework. If the obstacle leads to a practical problem, then the 'PRACTICE' framework can be employed. However, it may be that while the coachee has neither a practical problem nor an EP about this adversity, its presence may mean that the coachee has neither the time nor the focus to continue in coaching for the time being and a break from coaching may be indicated. Here, the coach invites the coachee to resume the process when the person has both the time and the mental space to devote to pursuing their coaching objectives.

- An internal adversity occurs that is related to the REBC process (e.g. the coachee begins to avoid doing tasks that they need to carry out to achieve their goal and there is no external reason for this avoidance).

This is usually indicative of an EP that can be dealt with by the coach using the 'Situational ABCDEFG' framework. However, if it transpires that this is due to a practical problem, then the 'PRACTICE' framework can be employed.

- The coachee encounters an environmental change that threatens the continuation of the REBC process (e.g. the coachee has taken on a lot more work to cover for a sick colleague).

Here, the coach can help the coachee by using the 'PRACTICE' framework to determine whether they can find a way of dealing with the environmental change. If not, this may mean that the coachee postpones coaching until they have the time to devote to it.

EPF-REBC: Step 17. Strategy 2. How to deal with an EP about an EP

One common obstacle that is worthy of mention here is when the person has an EP about their original EP and the presence of this 'meta-EP'[10] means that the person cannot focus sufficiently on their 'primary' EP. When this occurs, the REB coach helps the coachee in the following way:

- Agree with the coachee to focus on the meta-EP.
- Assess a specific example of the meta-EP.
- Focus on the problematic emotional, behavioural and cognitive responses at 'C'. Shame is a common meta-EP, for example.
- Identify the 'A'. Discover what the coachee found particularly disturbing about the primary EP. This could be the feelings or sensations the person experienced or the meaning of the problem for the coachee (e.g. "Having this problem is evidence that I have a weakness").
- Identify the coachee's goal. Encourage them to strive towards healthy ways of responding to the original EP.
- Identify the REAs the person held towards their original EP and their alternative FNAs.
- Help the coachee dispute both sets of beliefs.
- Encourage the coachee to rehearse and act in ways that are consistent with their developing FNAs towards their original EP until they are ready to return to dealing with it free from the obstructing effects of the meta-EP.

[At one point, Sarah made herself unhealthily angry about her propensity to feel guilt. She saw her guilt as ridiculous and demanded that she not be ridiculous. This served as an obstacle to progress and thus became a focus of what might be termed 'obstacle-focused coaching'. Thus, Sarah's coach encouraged her to think temporarily that it was ridiculous to feel guilt under these circumstances and helped her to develop the flexible attitude that, while this may be so, she was not immune as a human being from being ridiculous and nor does she have to have such immunity. This helped Sarah to get the situation into perspective and she began to view her guilt in a more realistic and compassionate manner.]

EPF-REBC: Step 18. Invite the coachee to consider development-focused REBC once they have achieved their EPF goal

Once the coachee has concluded EPF-REBC to their satisfaction, then the coach can ask the coachee if they wish to nominate a development-based coaching objective or end the process at this point. When the coachee is 'under the influence' of their EP(s), they are not able to focus on the issue of how they might like to develop themself as a person in one or more life areas. However, freed from such 'influence', they can better focus on this question and, at this point, they should be given the opportunity of doing so by their REB coach.

If the coachee agrees, then the coaching contract is modified to reflect this major shift of emphasis.

[This is what Sarah's coach said: "Now you have effectively addressed your feelings of guilt about acting selfishly, I wonder if you would like me to help you to develop yourself as a person in any area of your life?" Sarah said that she would and a description of this work appears in Chapter 4.]

3 A step-based framework for the practice of practical problem-focused REBC (PPF-REBC)

In this section, I will deal with the steps that the REB coach is called upon to make when their coachee is seeking help for a practical problem (PP) or problems. When a coachee has a PP, they tend to be confused or tangled up with an issue (or issues) and need some clarity and order, which they hope to get by talking things through with the coach. While they may be dissatisfied about the issue, they are not emotionally disturbed about it, although this should be verified by the coach (see the 'PPF-REBC: Step 1. Strategy 3' section). In these circumstances, the basic tasks of the REB coach are to help the coachee order their thoughts, define the problem in a way that is solvable, then set goals with respect to this problem and utilise the best methods to solve the problem. There are many practical problem-solving frameworks in the psychological literature. In this book, I will make use of the one devised by Palmer (2008) – 'PRACTICE' – because it was developed specifically for use in coaching (see Table 4 for an overview).

PPF-REBC: Step 1. Help the coachee to identify the problem ('problem identification' in the PRACTICE framework)

When a coachee seeks coaching for a PP, they are either clear about the nature of the problem or not. PPF-REBC proceeds differently in these two cases.

PPF-REBC: Step 1. Strategy 1. When the coachee's problem is clear

When the coachee says that they are clear about the problem, then the coach asks them to state the problem as specifically as they can, helping them to be concrete if they give vague responses. Asking for a

Table 4: The PRACTICE problem-solving framework (adapted from Palmer, 2008)

P	Problem identification
R	Realistic, relevant goal development
A	Alternative potential solutions generated
C	Consideration of potential solutions
T	Target most feasible potential solution
I	Implementation of chosen potential solution
C	Consolidation of the chosen potential solution
E	Evaluation

specific example of the problem, if relevant, is useful here. As noted in the 'EPF-REBC: Step 2. Strategy 1' section, such an example occurs in a specific situation, at a specific time, and with specific people present, with your coachee either behaving in a certain way or wanting to act in a certain way, but inhibiting themself from doing so.

The coach's questions to the coachee at this point can be about the situation (e.g. "What was problematic for you about the situation that you were in?") or about their response to the situation (e.g. "What was problematic about the way you responded (or did not respond) in the situation?").

The purpose of the coach's questions is for coach and coachee to understand the problem and to come up with an agreed problem statement (e.g. "My problem is that I find it hard to organise my workday").

PPF-REBC: Step 1. Strategy 2. When the coachee is confused about the problem

When the coachee is confused about the problem, the coach's goal is to help them to gain clarity before identifying the problem as above. The coach does this initially by encouraging the coachee to talk about what they are confused about and listening for ways to ask questions designed to help the coachee be more specific in their responses (e.g. "Can you be more specific about that?" "Can you help me understand what is problematic for you about that?" "How do you think someone who did not have a problem would deal with that?"). Once the coach has helped the coachee gain clarity, then they can ask for more specific examples of the problem and proceed in the way already outlined above.

PPF-REBC: Step 1. Strategy 3. Check for the existence of an EP about the PP and proceed accordingly

Even though the coach has embarked on PPF-REBC because the coachee has stated that the nature of the problem is practical rather than emotional in nature, it is useful to verify that this is the case. The best time to do this is when the coach and coachee have clearly identified the problem.

Here, the coach can ask such questions as, "How do you feel about your difficulty in organising your workday?" Answers that show that the coachee is experiencing a HNE about the problem (such as concern, disappointment and healthy anger) indicate they the person has a realistic and healthy response to the PP and the coaching can continue along PPF-REBC lines. However, replies that show that the coachee is experiencing a UNE (e.g. anxiety, shame and unhealthy anger) indicate that the person has an unhealthy response to the PP.

In this latter case, the coach needs to offer the coachee a plausible rationale as to why they should ideally tackle the EP about the PP before addressing the PP itself. The coach helps the coachee to appreciate that they have more chance in solving their PP when they have dealt with this EP than when they haven't. If the coachee still wishes to address their PP first, then the coach is advised to go along with this and switch to the EP if its existence does prove to be an obstacle.

> *[James sought coaching because he was struggling with his finances. He was constantly "chasing his tail," as he put it, and was always "in the red" at the end of the month. His parents reluctantly helped him get back "into the black," but neither James nor his parents wanted this to be a permanent solution to the problem. James was a good candidate for PPF-REBC because while he was disappointed about the situation and wanted to address it, he was not emotionally disturbed about it.]*

PPF-REBC: Step 2. Help the coachee to set goals ('realistic, relevant goal development' in the PRACTICE framework)

Once the coach has helped the coachee to identify their target problem, it is important to help them to set a goal. The REB coach uses the well-known acronym 'SMART' to help their coachee to set goals. This acronym stands for specific, measurable, achievable, relevant and time-bound.

PPF-REBC: Step 2. Strategy 1. Help the coachee to set a goal that is specific

Such a goal specifies the criteria whereby the coachee will regard the problem as solved.

PPF-REBC: Step 2. Strategy 2. Help the coachee to develop a goal that is measurable

Here, the coach encourages the coachee to devise a way of measuring their progress towards their goal and also when it has been achieved.

PPF-REBC: Step 2. Strategy 3. Ensure that the goal is achievable

By an achievable goal, I mean two things here: first, a goal that is achievable is one that is within the power of the coachee to achieve; and second, an achievable goal is one that is realistic given the resources that the coachee has at their disposal.

PPF-REBC: Step 2. Strategy 4. Ensure that the goal is relevant to the coachee

A relevant goal is one that, if achieved, will make a real difference to the coachee given where they currently are in their life with respect to the problem.

PPF-REBC: Step 2. Strategy 5. Help the coachee to set a realistic timeline within which they will achieve their goal

It is important that the coach determines with the coachee how much time they have to achieve their goal since the amount of time at the coachee's disposal will have a significant influence on the goal that they choose. It is also important for the coach to help the coachee to agree with themself as to how much time they plan to spend on goal-related tasks. Thus, a coachee who is going to devote a large chunk of time to regular goal-directed activity can afford to be more ambitious in goal-setting than the coachee who is only going to devote a small chunk of time to infrequent goal-directed activity.

[James' goal was to be 'in the black' at the end of the month. He knew that this was achievable because he earned a good salary, but claimed that he did not know where all his money went. Encouraged to be more specific by his coach, James said his goal was to put £50 into a savings account at the end of each month. In order to discover the extent of the problem, James agreed to keep a detailed account of his monthly outgoings and what he spent in that period. James expressed surprise that he never considered doing this before since it "seemed so obvious."]

The coachee is now ready to use the rest of the 'PRACTICE' model having been helped to identify their PP and set goals. In doing so, the coach can help the coachee to identify previous successful attempts at solving similar PPs and to examine their relevance to dealing with the target problem.

PPF-REBC: Step 3. Help the coachee to develop possible solutions to the problem ('alternative potential solutions generated' in the PRACTICE framework)

Before helping the coachee to generate potential solutions to the problem, it is important that the coach finds out how the person has previously attempted to tackle the problem.

PPF-REBC: Step 3. Strategy 1. Assess previous problem-solving attempts

It is very likely that what the coachee has already tried in order to solve the problem has not proven effective; after all, they have come for coaching help to solve the problem. However, it is important that the coach knows what these previous attempts are so that they don't end up encouraging the coachee to do something that they have already tried that has proven not to work. Also, there may be certain elements of what the coachee has tried that were useful and it is important that the coach knows about these so that they can build on these elements rather than starting from scratch.

PPF-REBC: Step 3. Strategy 2. Initiate brainstorming

Once previous attempts to solve the problem have been identified and 'mined' for their productive elements (which can be filed away for later use), the coach encourages the brainstorming of possible solutions to the problem. Brainstorming is a useful strategy designed to encourage the coachee to be creative in their thinking, free from the concern that they will come up with something silly or stupid, for example. Indeed, the coach might join in this process by modelling the free and unconstrained thinking that they are trying to encourage in the coachee. It often happens that the brainstorming yields an effective potential solution to the coachee's problem that they would not have thought of otherwise.

[After keeping a monthly log of his expenditure and outgoings, James and his coach could clearly see where the problem lay. James was spending what he said was "far too much buying drinks for my friends in the pub." He and his coach brainstormed possible solutions to this problem. These were:

1. *Stopping going to the pub altogether.*
2. *Going to the pub once a week.*
3. *Going to the pub as often, only buying one round a week, but not explaining the reasons for the change of behaviour to my friends.*
4. *Going to the pub as often, only buying one round per evening and explaining the reasons for this change of behaviour to my friends.]*

PPF-REBC: Step 4. Help the coachee to evaluate these potential solutions ('consideration of potential solutions' in the PRACTICE framework)

Once the coachee has completed the process of generating potential solutions, it is time for them to consider and evaluate each one.

PPF-REBC: Step 4. Strategy 1. Help the coachee to consider the likely consequences of each solution

At this point, the main emphasis in PPF-REBC is on the likely consequences of implementing each possible solution (Palmer, 2008). This is an important consideration because, after all, the coachee has come for help with solving their problem(s). When considering the consequences of potential solutions, the coach not only needs to help the coachee think of the effectiveness of each possible solution with respect to its problem-solving potential, they also need to help them think of other consequences as well (e.g. the impact of the potential solution on others involved in that area of the coachee's life and the longer-term effects of solving the problem using the approach selected to do so).

PPF-REBC: Step 4. Strategy 2. Help the coachee to think of their values when considering potential solutions

In addition to the likely consequences of each potential solution, the coach needs to help the coachee consider the relationship between a potential solution and the coachee's *values*. Thus, from a pragmatic perspective, the coachee may have generated a potential solution with the best chance of solving their problem, but implementing it might compromise one or more of their values and therefore they might hold back from selecting this potential solution as one to try out.

PPF-REBC: Step 4. Strategy 3. Help the coachee to consider whether they have the skills and/or capability to implement the potential solutions

Another issue concerns whether or not the coachee has the necessary capability, in the first place, or the necessary skills, in the second place, to carry out a potential solution that they consider to have the best chance of solving their problem if implemented. If the coachee does not have the capability to implement a potential solution, then the matter is clear: the coachee won't be able to implement it. However, if they don't have the skills (but they do have the capability) to do so, then the coach will need to discuss with them whether it is worth it to them to learn the requisite skills in order to implement the chosen potential solution. The greater the number of plausible and potentially effective solutions that are available to the coachee, the less likely it is that they will choose to learn the aforementioned skills. However, if the chosen potential solution is the only feasible solution, then they probably will choose to learn the skills to implement it. If the coach can teach the coachee such skills themselves, then they should do so, but, if not, then they should help the coachee source the necessary training elsewhere.

[James came up with following concerning each of his brainstormed potential solutions:

- Stop going to the pub altogether. *This would solve the problem, but would deprive me of one of my pleasures in life – drinking regularly with my friends – I am not prepared to do this.*
- Going to the pub once a week. *This is a less extreme version of the above and not really acceptable to me.*
- Going to the pub as often, only buying one round a week, but not explaining the reasons for the change of behaviour to my friends. *This is a better solution, but my friends would wonder what I had suddenly changed. I'm not being honest.*
- Going to the pub as often, only buying one round per evening and explaining the reasons for this change of behaviour to my friends. *This is also a better solution and one where I am being honest and my friends will see where I am coming from, but they will 'rib' me about it for weeks.]*

PPF-REBC: Step 5. Help the coachee to select the best solution ('target the most feasible potential solution' in the PRACTICE framework)

At the end of the consideration process described above, the coachee should, ideally, be in a position to select one or sometimes more potential solutions that they hope will actually solve their problem. If more than one solution is chosen, the coachee should then rank them in the order that they will use them. The first on the list is known as the 'target solution'. If this turns out not to be effective, then the coach should encourage the coachee to select the next one on the list and so on.

[James decided to opt for the following as his target solution: 'Going to the pub as often, only buying one round per evening and explaining

the reasons for this change of behaviour to his friends'. His reasons were as follows:

1. I enjoy going to the pub and I don't want to go less often.
2. I want to gain control of my spending and so buying one round per evening will definitely help.
3. Explaining to my friends why I am limiting myself to buying one round per evening will give them a rationale for my behaviour and, although they will 'rib' me, I hope they will also support me.]

PPF-REBC: Step 6. Help the coachee to put the target solution into practice ('implementation of the chosen potential solution' in the PRACTICE framework)

Once the coachee has selected a target potential solution, they need help with implementing it. Several issues need to be considered when the coach and coachee discuss the implementation of their target potential solution.

PPF-REBC: Step 6. Strategy 1. Help the coachee to break the target solution into manageable sub-tasks

Sometimes the target solution may later be dismissed by a coachee because it seems too complex. To ensure that this does not happen, it is useful for the coach to help the coachee to break it down into manageable sub-tasks. This will also help when the coachee comes to implementing the solution.

PPF-REBC: Step 6. Strategy 2. Help the coachee to decide when to implement the target solution's sub-tasks, where and, if relevant, with whom

I earlier argued that it was important to help the coachee to be specific when carrying out homework tasks designed to solve their EP (see the 'EPF-REBC: Step 13. Strategy 7' section). This is also the case when the coachee's problem is practical in nature. The coachee should be asked to specify when they will carry out the target solution's sub-tasks, in which situations and with which other people if the help of these people is integral to the solution.

PPF-REBC: Step 6. Strategy 3. Help the coachee to identify potential obstacles to the implementation of the target solution and deal with these before they become actual obstacles

See the 'EPF-REBC: Step 16' section.

> *[James put into practice his target solution and reported back that on the first occasion he did so it went quite well, although one of his friends was quite abusive and accused him of being mean. James and his coach discussed this and James decided to persist and risk losing the man's friendship if he continued being rude.]*

PPF-REBC: Step 7. Help the coachee to embed the chosen solution ('consolidation of the chosen potential solution' in the PRACTICE framework)

It is quite rare for a coachee to solve their problem the first time they implement their chosen potential solution.

PPF-REBC: Step 7. Strategy 1. Help the coachee to give the target solution a fair chance to work

Given the above point, the coach should ask the coachee to answer the following question: "How am I going to ensure that I have given the target solution the best chance to see if it yields the results I want?" If the coachee implements their answer to this question, then this will ensure that they have utilised the actual potency of their target solution to effect the change that they seek and thus to assess its effectiveness.

PPF-REBC: Step 7. Strategy 2. Help the coachee to discuss their experiences of implementing the target solution and make modifications to it, if necessary

During this process, the coach should discuss with the coachee their experiences of implementation of their target solution. This will help the coachee to make any modifications to the potential solution that they are carrying out and how they are executing it. It also gives both coach and coachee another opportunity to identify and discuss dealing with any actual obstacles the coachee encounters during this phase of PPF-REBC (again, see the 'EPF-REBC: Step 16' section).

[James continued to implement his target solution and although he did lose the friendship of the person who was rude to him as this rudeness continued, it turned out that James' other friends supported him and the person concerned stopped coming to the pub.]

PPF-REBC: Step 8. Help the coachee to evaluate the target solution ('evaluation' in the PRACTICE framework)

When the coachee has implemented the target solution over the selected consolidation period, the coach needs to help them to evaluate its effects. Has it solved the problem? If not, does it look like it has the potential to solve the problem given more implementation time? If so, then the coach should encourage the coachee to carry on with the chosen problem-solving tasks. If not, the coach should encourage them to select the next potential solution from their list and use the same steps as above. The coach and coachee should process in this way until the problem has been solved. If it is still not solved, it may be that the coachee has an EP about the PP that has not been identified despite initial efforts to do so and a more detailed assessment of the possible existence of such a problem needs to be done. If such a problem is found, then PPF-REBC becomes EPF-REBC and the steps that I outlined when discussing EPF-REBC should be followed and its strategies implemented.

[By implementing his target solution, James saved more than the £50 he had set as his monthly savings target and was no longer in debt. At this point, James terminated coaching two months after commencing. He had maintained his goal three months later.]

PPF-REBC: Step 9. Invite the coachee to consider development-focused REBC once they have achieved their PPF goal

See the 'EPF-REBC: Step 18' section for a discussion of this issue.

[After achieving what he came to coaching to achieve, James decided not to opt for development-focused REBC.]

4 A step-based framework for the practice of development-focused REBC (DF-REBC)

The major purpose of DF-REBC is to help the coachee to get the most out of themselves in whichever life area that they nominate. The person should not be experiencing an EP when embarking on DF-REBC. If they are, EPF-REBC should be offered and completed before DF-REBC gets underway.

DF-REBC: Step 1. Introduce the concept of healthy principles of living as the foundation of DF-REBC

The main feature of DF-REBC that sets it apart from problem-focused REBC (PF-REBC) is its emphasis on growth and development. What underpins the practice of DF-REBC is REBC's concept of healthy principles of living.[1] These principles are "the essential ingredients of a philosophy of personal happiness that Ellis[2] provides for people to help them to live enjoyable, enriched, satisfying and pleasurable lives" (Bernard, 2011: 2). In Appendix 1, I present a survey that I developed to help coachees in DF-REBC. Bernard (2018a) has presented a survey that he devised entitled the 'Rationality and Happiness Survey' where he outlines and describes 11 principles of rational living. Such surveys can be used to help the coachee review how present such principles are in their life, how important such principles are and how they might underpin the selection of development-based objectives.

DF-REBC: Step 1. Strategy 1. Help the coachee to review the presence of healthy principles in their life

One of the ways in which a survey of healthy (or rational) principles of living can be used in DF-REBC is to encourage the coachee to review how present such principles are in their life. This can serve as a platform for a conversation between coach and coachee concerning how the coachee views their development, the role of such principles in their development and the place of these principles in coaching.

DF-REBC: Step 1. Strategy 2. Help the coachee to choose how to use these principles in DF-REBC

These healthy principles of living can be used in DF-REBC in two main ways:

1. First, they can be used as broad objectives that the coachee selects because they think that it is important for their development that they are more self-accepting, for example, in which case the coach helps the coachee to identify more specific markers of such broad objectives (e.g. "What specifically would tell you that you were more accepting of yourself", "What objectives would you like to nominate that would indicate that you were more self-accepting?"). When the principles are used in this way, they can be regarded as '*drivers*' in DF-REBC in that they drive the process by influencing the selection of coaching objectives.
2. Second, healthy principles can be used as '*mediators*' in DF-REBC. Here, the coachee first selects an objective that is important to them and then chooses a principle that will aid the pursuit of the objective. The coachee reminds themself of the principle while they are pursuing the objective. For example, consider a person who wants to develop their leadership skills and has selected 'risk-taking' as a mediating principle. When tempted to play safe in a situation that calls upon them to use their developing leadership skills, the person reminds themself that they need to take a risk and does so. This is an example of how the objective drives the selection of the principle, which is then employed for its mediating, motivational properties.

The coach can explain to the coachee the two ways of using healthy principles of living in DF-REBC and then the two of them can have a more specific conversation concerning the best way in which these principles can inform that person's coaching.

[If you recall from Chapter 2, Sarah decided to accept her coach's offer to move into DF-REBC once she had achieved her goals from EPF-REBC. At the outset, her coach outlined to Sarah the two approaches to using the healthy principles of living in DF-REBC and Sarah decided to use her selected principles as mediating motivators (see above). These principles were 'enlightened self-interest' and 'discomfort tolerance'.]

DF-REBC: Step 2. Help the coachee to set objectives[3]

While REBC emphasises specificity, the concept of development does tend to be quite broad and experiential. "I will know when I feel it" is the kind of language that a coachee may use when discussing how they will know when they have achieved their development-based objectives. Thus, skilled REB coaches are able to marry the specific and evidential with the general and experiential when helping coachees to set development-based objectives. In what follows, I outline some important strategies that will aid the objective-setting process.[4]

DF-REBC: Step 2. Strategy 1. Help the coachee to understand the attributes of a development-based objective in DF-REBC

When discussing a development-based objective with a coachee, the REB coach keeps in mind and helps the coachee to see that that a 'good' objective in DF-REBC has the following features:

- It has a direction.
- It may be ongoing (thus it may not have an end-point).
- When it does have an end-point, this often needs to be maintained. For example, if a coachee wants to enhance their competent communication skills at work, this indicates a direction and, if an end-point can be specified, it will have to be maintained. The same is true, for example, with goals that involve improvements in physical fitness or eating. Indeed, if one stops working on either of these latter areas when targets have been reached, then a return to 'square one' will eventually occur.
- A development-based objective is broad with specific referents (see the 'PPF-REBC: Step 2' section).

DF-REBC: Step 2. Strategy 2. Help the coachee to choose an objective that has intrinsic rather than extrinsic importance for them

It is important for the coachee to select an objective that they want to achieve rather than what a stakeholder[5] wants them to achieve. However, if the coach and stakeholder both want the same thing for the coachee, then this is particularly helpful for the REBC process.

DF-REBC: Step 2. Strategy 3. Help the coachee to choose an objective that rests on a principle of healthy psychological living prized by the coachee

If the coachee has several development-based coaching objectives in mind, then the concept of healthy principles of living discussed earlier may be useful in helping the coachee to select a target objective (i.e. the objective that the coachee wishes to pursue first) that is based on a particularly prized healthy principle.

DF-REBC: Step 2. Strategy 4. Help the coachee to choose an objective that is underpinned by values that are important to the coachee

A value is the coachee's judgement of what is important or meaningful in their life or gives purpose to that life. I use terms like 'meaning', 'importance' or 'purpose' if coachees don't resonate with the term 'value'. Many development-based objectives are pragmatic (i.e. they lead to useful benefits for the individual; e.g. a salary rise or career advancement) and there is nothing wrong with that. However, a coachee is less likely to persist in the pursuit of pragmatic objectives that are not also underpinned by values than they would if this value-based foundation is present. If a coachee requests help in determining their values, I suggest that they complete an online test at www.value-test.com.[6]

DF-REBC: Step 2. Strategy 5. Help the coachee to choose an objective that preferably involves tasks that have intrinsic merit for the coachee

The more that the coachee enjoys the tasks that they need to do in order to achieve their development-based objective, the better, as they are more likely to engage with such tasks than when they are not enjoyable. However, if these tasks do not have intrinsic merit for the coachee, they can still do them while keeping in mind that it is good for them to do these unpleasant tasks because they will help them achieve what they want. I call this the 'cod liver oil' principle.[7]

DF-REBC: Step 2. Strategy 6. Help the coachee to choose an objective that they are prepared to integrate into their life

The coachee may select an intrinsic, meaningful objective that expresses a valued healthy principle of living that is enjoyable to pursue, but if the person cannot integrate this objective into their life, then there is no point in helping them to pursue it. This is why it is very important for the coach to help the coachee look at the place of the objective within the context of their life as a whole. If the objective is highly valued by the coachee but cannot, at present, be integrated into the person's life, the coach should invite the person to think about whether they want to restructure their life to accommodate the objective. If so, then the restructuring should take place first to accommodate the objective. If not, then the coach should invite the coachee to select an objective that can be integrated into their life.

DF-REBC: Step 2. Strategy 7. Help the coachee to choose an objective for which they are prepared to make sacrifices to achieve

If the coachee is prepared to restructure their life to accommodate their valued development-based objective, then the coach needs to help the coachee consider what changes they are prepared to make to do this. In all probability, this means the coachee being prepared to make sacrifices to achieve this. The more the coachee is prepared to make selected sacrifices, the more they will be willing to pursue their desired objective. It is important that the coach explores with the coachee the implications for making the selected sacrifices on other people in the person's life. It is important that other people are told of the sacrifice and what it might mean for them so that they can give their consent to the subsequent change for them. Indeed, if these other people can support the coachee both in making the sacrifice and in their pursuit of the objective, then this can be particularly helpful for the coachee.

Once the coach and coachee have agreed on a development-based objective, the next stage in development-focused REBC is to help them to devise an action plan and to implement it. In brief, designing a plan involves the coach helping the coachee to determine *what* they are going to do to achieve their development-based objective, while implementing the plan involves helping them to determine *how* they are going to put their action plan into practice.

[Sarah set as her coaching objective 'pursuing her own projects rather than doing things to make people happy'. She identified two specific markers for this objective: (i) learning to play the bassoon; and (ii) experimenting sexually with women. She decided to begin with playing the bassoon.]

DF-REBC: Step 3. Help the coachee to design an action plan

When helping the coachee to devise an action plan with respect to reaching their development-based objective, it is important for the coach to take the following steps.

DF-REBC: Step 3. Strategy 1. Help the coachee to devise a clear method for measuring for their development-based objective

As I said at the beginning of this section on DF-REBC, while a development-based objective may be broad, it is important that it has specific referents (e.g. the enactment of a specific leadership skill in a specific situation when the person broadly wants to improve their leadership skills). These help the coachee not only to know when they have achieved the objective, if relevant, but also to gauge their progress towards the objective. Once the coachee has met their objective, then, again if relevant, it is important to ask them how they will know precisely if they are maintaining it. These tasks require that the coach and coachee work together to devise a measure of tracking the coachee's progress towards the objective and their maintenance of the objective once achieved. While it is best if this measure provides specific information, some coachees prefer a more general, experiential-based measure. The coach should respect the coachee's wishes in this respect.

DF-REBC: Step 3. Strategy 2. Help the coachee to list the actions that they need to take to achieve the objective

The next step is to help the coachee to specify what actions they need to take to achieve the objective. In doing so, it is important to help them select actions that they already have the skills to perform. If they lack a skill that they need, the coach decides with them how they are going to learn it and from whom. On this point, it is important for the coach to realise that it is not their job to teach skills that they don't have in their own skills repertoire. However, it is their job to help the coachee to find the right resource in this respect. If the coach can teach a relevant skill to their coachee, they should do so.

DF-REBC: Step 3. Strategy 3. Help the coachee to construct a realistic time schedule to achieve their objective

This schedule will be determined partly based on the length of the coaching contract and on how many objectives the coachee wishes to set and work towards during the coaching process. Once the coachee has determined the time schedule, they should be helped to allocate tasks to time slots so that both coach and coachee know what the latter plans to do by when. This will need to be monitored and modified based on the coachee's actual experience of implementing the action plan.

DF-REBC: Step 3. Strategy 4. Help the coachee to use their strengths and other helping resources

When helping the coachee devise an action plan, they should be encouraged to use their strengths and other resources that they identified earlier (see the 'LTF: Step 3. Strategy 2' and the 'LTF: Step 3. Strategy 3' sections).

DF-REBC: Step 3. Strategy 5. Ensure that the coachee can integrate the action plan into their life

In the way that the coach helped the coachee ensure that they could integrate their development-based objective into their life, the coach should do the same with respect to their constructed action plan. Thus, when the coachee integrates this plan into their life, it means that they commit themself to act at particular times that are convenient to them and in contexts that are accessible. If this is not the case, the coach should help them to make modifications so that their action plan fits into their life.

DF-REBC: Step 3. Strategy 6. Suggest a launch date to the coachee who should decide whether to inform others

The coach might suggest to the coachee that they may wish to set a launch date for implementing their action plan and, if this resonates

50 Framework for the practice of DF-REBC

with the person, discuss what this might involve and whether they want to 'go public' with this. If this does not appeal to the coachee, have them begin as they wish.

[Sarah devised the following action plan in relation to learning to play the bassoon:

1. *Buying a bassoon.*
2. *Soundproofing her flat.*
3. *Finding a teacher that she feels comfortable with.*
4. *Booking a series of lessons.*
5. *Devising a practice schedule.*
6. *Joining an orchestra when proficient.]*

DF-REBC: Step 3. Strategy 7. Remind the coachee to use their selected rational principle(s) of living in designing the action plan

Rational principles of living can be used by the coachee throughout development-based REBC. In helping the person design the plan, the coach can suggest that the coachee keeps their selected rational principles of living at the front of their mind when doing so. Thus, a coachee can think of the principle of risk-taking when designing an action plan and perhaps be more adventurous in the design of that plan in order to reflect their wish to use risk-taking as a mediating variable in coaching.

DF-REBC: Step 4. Help the coachee to implement the action plan

When the coachee has launched their action plan, the coach has several tasks to perform in order to help them to stay on course towards their development-based objective.

DF-REBC: Step 4. Strategy 1. Encourage the coachee to use a selection of motivating variables

While the coachee is implementing their action plan, it is helpful for them to use one or more motivating variable(s) to sustain this implementation. Thus, the coachee can remind themself periodically of the importance of the objective in their life (e.g. "I am doing this because I want to improve my presentation skills"). Alternatively, they can select a healthy principle of living to keep in mind while pursuing the objective (see the 'DF-REBC: Step 1. Strategy 2' section). This can be done in two ways: first, it can be used as an outcome variable (e.g. "Doing this will help me be more creative in life"); and second, it can be used to deal with potential obstacles (e.g. "Even if I fail today, I'm not a failure. I'm fallible and I can learn from failure").

[Sarah chose the following as motivators: (a) "I have the right to play whatever musical instrument I want to learn even if people disapprove"; and (b) "I am going to persist with this no matter how hard it is."]

DF-REBC: Step 4. Strategy 2. Monitor the coachee's implementation of the action plan

The time–action schedule the coachee has developed (see above) is not one that is set in stone and will need to be changed in light of the coachee's experiences. Consequently, it is important that the coach monitors their progress on this. Such monitoring involves both coach and coachee being clear about what the latter is going to do, as mentioned above, and reviewing what they did, exploring the meaning of any discrepancies between plans and achievements. Any changes to the coachee's action plan should emerge out of their experiences of implementing it and any difficulties should be addressed.

[Sarah implemented her action plan as above, but found it difficult to find the right teacher. However, she persisted with this and eventually found one who she felt comfortable with and who was very patient, a quality Sarah discovered was important to her while speaking to several prospective bassoon teachers. She booked a series of lessons with her chosen teacher and kept to her devised practice schedule.]

DF-REBC: Step 4. Strategy 3. Help the coachee to capitalise on success

When it is clear that the coachee is doing well with respect to their action plan, it is important for the coach to help them to capitalise on their success. One way of doing this is to find out what it is that they have been doing that has brought about their progress and to suggest that they continue to do what is working for them (Iveson, George &

Ratner, 2012). Another way is to encourage them to think of ways that they can generalise what they have been learning from implementing their development-based objective to other relevant areas of their life where they would like to develop themself.

DF-REBC: Step 4. Strategy 4. Help the coachee to maintain their gains once they have met their objective

Once the coachee has achieved their objective, it is probable that they will have to take action to maintain the gains that they have obtained. Thus, it is important that the coach works with the coachee on the following issues:

- Help them to identify and implement steps they will need to take in order to maintain their gains.
- Help them to identify and deal with any obstacles that might interfere with such maintenance strategies (see the 'EPF-REBC: Step 16' section).

[Sarah had what she called a 'wobble' when two of her relatives made fun of her when they found out that she was learning to play the bassoon. Her coach used the 'Situational ABCDEFG' framework to help her deal with her feelings of shame that had led her to give up the bassoon for two weeks. As Sarah was familiar with this framework, she was able to use it to good effect so that she resumed bassoon practice and lessons after addressing her feelings of shame and asserting herself with her relatives.]

- Help them to develop tolerance for the discomfort and boredom that they might experience during the maintenance process.
- Help them identify and deal with any vulnerability factors that, if encountered, might lead them to experience lapses in the use of their maintenance strategies that, in turn, may result in the loss of gains already achieved from DF-REBC.

DF-REBC: Step 4. Strategy 5. Help the coachee to pursue other objectives and generalise learning

Once the coachee has shown evidence of maintaining their target development-based objective, they are ready to pursue another objective (if relevant). The coach can help them go through the same process with the new objective, informed by the work that they have done on the first objective. As they make progress on the second objective, the coach can encourage the coachee to: (a) look for patterns amongst the objectives that they have nominated at the outset; and (b) use these patterns as they increasingly take on the role of being their own coach.

The more the coach can help the coachee to identify and use productive patterns of thinking and acting from the work they have done with them on their objectives, the more the coach can help them to formalise these as self-development principles and generalise them across different life domains. These principles would include both some of the healthy principles outlined in Appendix 1, but put in the coachee's own words, and other principles that fall outside this list.

[Although it was a very different area, Sarah capitalised on her success at learning the bassoon in order to begin to explore her sexuality by dating women. This proved very successful and not as uncomfortable as she had predicted, so she decided after a few months to come out as 'bisexual'. Interestingly, her mother was much more accepting of her than she had predicted, although she faced hostility from the same two relatives who had criticised her decision to learn to play the bassoon. However, armed with her new attitudes based on enlightened self-interest and unconditional self-acceptance, she was disappointed but not hurt by their criticism.]

In the final chapter, I will consider the issues of ending coaching, follow-up and evaluation.

5 Ending REBC, follow-up and evaluation (EFE)

EFE: Step 1. Ending the REBC process

Once a coachee has made progress in achieving and maintaining some or most of their development-based objectives and problem-based goals, shown evidence that they can generalise their learning to other life areas and can, in some important ways, carry on the coaching process for themself, then it may be time to discuss how the coachee and coach are going to end the process.

EFE: Step 1. Strategy 1. Discuss and decide on an agreed approach to ending

It is important that the coach and coachee discuss a mutually agreed way of ending the process. Of course, the ending may have already been specified at the outset in the coaching contract the coach made with their coachee, but if this is not the case, then the issue should be formally placed on the coaching agenda by one or both parties, preferably well before the formal end of the process. Often the REB coach and the coachee agree to meet less often as the latter makes progress towards their objectives and wishes to become more autonomous in the process. Thus, there is no one correct way to end REBC. Rather, the ending needs to be a 'good one' and that is most likely to occur when it has been fully discussed and agreed between the coach and coachee.

EFE: Step 1. Strategy 2. Encourage the coachee to summarise the process

At the final session, it is important for the coach to give the coachee an opportunity to summarise what has occurred in the process and what they learned from it. The coach's role here is basically a listening, clarifying one and perhaps to prompt the coachee to focus on any areas not covered by their summary and learning statement. The coach should place particular emphasis on helping the coachee to specify the healthy principles of living that they have learned and/or strengthened that they can take forwards into their lives. It is also important for the coach to give the coachee an opportunity to raise any matters of unfinished business and help the coachee to gain closure. The coach should also seek feedback from the coach concerning what was valuable about the process and what was not helpful if these issues have not been covered by the coachee's summary and learning statement.

Finally, the coach should discuss with the coachee the issues of follow-up and evaluation.

EFE: Step 2. Follow-up

REB coaches conduct a follow-up session for the following reasons:

1. Follow-up provides an opportunity for the coachee to give feedback on what they have done in the time between the last time they saw their coach and the follow-up session.
2. Knowing that there is a feedback session scheduled offers the coachee a sense of care and connection with their coach.
3. A follow-up session provides the coachee with an opportunity to request more coaching help if needed, whether this is development-focused or problem-focused.
4. Follow-up enables the coach and any organisation in which the coach works to carry out outcome evaluation (i.e. how the coachee has done). If the coach does this, then they will have to give some thought to how they are going to measure outcomes and what forms, if any, they are going to use.
5. Follow-up provides service evaluation data (what the coachee thought of the help provided) and such data will help the coach and any organisation in which they work to improve the service offered.

EFE: Step 2. Strategy 1. Agree a set time for the follow-up session with the coachee

While there is no set interval after the formal end of REBC in which the follow-up session should take place, the coach and coachee should agree on a definite time and ensure that this date is in their respective diaries. My own practice is to conduct the follow-up session three months after coaching has ended. However, the timing of this session will vary according to the coach, the service in which they work, if relevant, and the coachee.

EFE: Step 2. Strategy 2. Agree the follow-up format

While the format of the follow-up session is usually the same as the format of coaching (face to face or Skype or a similar platform), there is usually more flexibility in how the follow-up session is conducted. This is simply because the coachee in particular may not know where they are going to be on the date of the follow-up if it is scheduled a long-time in the future (e.g. three months).

EFE: Step 3. Evaluating outcomes

Different coaches will have different ways of evaluating their work and there is no one way of evaluating outcomes in REBC. It is important that the REB coach develops a way of evaluating their work that is consistent with their professional affiliation, satisfies their employer (if they are employed) and is relevant to their coachees.

EFE: Step 3. Strategy 1. One example of evaluating outcomes

My own approach to evaluating outcomes is to construct an individualised measure with my coachee to provide pre- and post-coaching data with respect to their development-based objectives or problem-based goals that also allows us to monitor the coachee's progress towards achieving these objectives or goals. Table 5 gives an example of one evaluation protocol that I have used that was developed for use over the telephone. It can be slightly modified for use as a questionnaire to be completed by the coachee.

In addition, the coach might ask the coachee to complete again the 'healthy principles of living' survey listed in Appendix 1 and see if any changes are apparent in the 'frequency of use' ratings provided by the coachee. This would provide subjective evaluation outcome data on the roles those principles play in REBC.

Table 5: Follow-up evaluation protocol*

1. We agreed the following objective/goal for coaching:

2. How successful have you been in achieving your objective or goal? Would you say that the status quo as it was then [*restate as described by the coachee*] is about the same or has changed? If changed, list it on a five-point scale as follows:

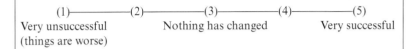

   (1)————(2)————(3)————(4)————(5)
   Very unsuccessful   Nothing has changed   Very successful
   (things are worse)

3. What do you think made the change (for better or worse) possible. If conditions are the same, ask "What makes it stay the same?"

4. If people around you have given you the feedback that you have changed, how do they think you have changed?

5. Which of the healthy principles of living that you discussed with your coach was most helpful in your coaching? Please elaborate.

6. Besides the specific issue of [*state the relevant area*], have there been other areas that have changed (for better or worse). If so, what?

7. Now please let me ask you a few questions about the coaching that you received. What do you recall from the sessions that you had?

8. What do you recall that was particularly helpful or unhelpful?

(*continued*)

58 Ending REBC, follow-up and evaluation

Table 5: (*Cont.*)

9. How satisfied are you with the coaching that you received? Use a five-point scale as follows: (1)————(2)————(3)————(4)————(5) Dissatisfied   Moderately   Extremely   satisfied   satisfied
10. Did you find the coaching package to be sufficient? If not, would you wish to resume coaching? Would you wish to change coach?
11. What recommendations for improvement in the service that you received do you have?
12. Is there anything else I have not specifically asked you that you would like me to know?

* This can also be used, with modifications, earlier to assess the person's progress in coaching

Having presented one approach to evaluating outcome, I refer the interested reader to Gray (2004) and Carter (2006) for an extended discussion of the issues concerning coaching evaluation.

[Sarah and her coach decided to have a follow-up session four months after DF-REBC ended. At that meeting, Sarah said that she had continued to go out weekly with her friends and on dates, leaving her mother on her own. Although her mother complained about this and although Sarah had the occasional "twinge of guilt," she kept to this "weekly going-out schedule," as she called it. She decided not to join an orchestra, but was happy to play for herself, her mother

and her new 'girlfriend' who she had just started dating. Sarah did not want to quantify what she had achieved from coaching, but did say that she now felt much more herself than at any other period of her life.]

This brings us to the end of the book. I hope you have found it valuable. If you have any feedback I would be grateful to receive it, c/o windy@windydryden.com

Appendix 1
20 healthy principles of living and development-focused coaching

1. On a scale from 1 to 5, with 1 representing 'never or hardly at all', 3 representing 'reasonably often' and 5 representing 'very often', indicate how frequently you make use of the following principles in your life.
2. List your coaching objectives if set.
   a)
   b)
   c)
   d)
3. Indicate with a '✓' if you think a particular principle should underpin your chosen coaching objective(s) or a '✗' if not. Write in the appropriate letter when referring to a particular objective (a, b, c, d).

Personal responsibility "While I recognise that events contribute to the way I feel and act, I am largely responsible for my emotion and behaviour."	Frequency rating: ✓ or ✗: a b c d
Flexible and non-extreme attitudes "My attitudes towards adversity and other issues are largely flexible and non-extreme rather than rigid and extreme."	Frequency rating: ✓ or ✗: a b c d

20 healthy principles

Scientific thinking "I think for myself rather than relying on the views of others. I test out my assumptions rather than regarding them as facts."	Frequency rating: ✓ or ✗: a b c d
Unconditional self-acceptance "While I recognise I have my faults and may need to improve in certain areas, I accept myself unconditionally as a fallible human being with strengths and weaknesses and tend not to devalue myself."	Frequency rating: ✓ or ✗: a b c d
Enlightened self-interest "I recognise that if I do not look after my own interest no-one else will and therefore most of the time I decide to put myself first and others a close second. However, at other times, I choose to put others' interests before my own."	Frequency rating: ✓ or ✗: a b c d
Accept others unconditionally "While I recognise that others have their faults and may need to improve in certain areas, I accept them unconditionally as fallible human beings with strengths and weaknesses and tend not to devalue them."	Frequency rating: ✓ or ✗: a b c d
Develop social interest "I recognise that I live in a social context and I show sensitivity to the interests of others. I will help others to further their interests as long as doing so does not interfere with me looking after my own healthy interests."	Frequency rating: ✓ or ✗: a b c d

Be self-directed while being mindful of the social context "Once I have set goals and have committed myself to pursuing them, I choose to do so while being mindful of my other commitments and the social context in which I live. While I will largely direct myself in this regard, this does not preclude me from seeking support from others when appropriate."	Frequency rating: ✓ or ✘: a b c d
Develop tolerance for uncertainty "While I prefer to be certain about matters that are important to me, I don't need such certainty. I can tolerate not knowing and recognise that in many areas of life certainty doesn't exist. Often, all we have is probability and I resolve to take a course of action that is probably the best one to take and accept the consequences of doing so. Being flexible rather than rigid about uncertainty helps me to see that uncertainty is not inevitably linked with a bad outcome."	Frequency rating: ✓ or ✘: a b c d
Take calculated risks "I recognise that playing safe is often the most comfortable option in the short term, but will not help me to realise my dreams in the longer term. I am prepared to take risks that I have carefully considered and will increase my chances of achieving these goals if I take them. However, I realise that taking such risks may not work out for me and I will accept this grim reality and will accept myself if I take an action that makes things worse for me. If the latter happens, I will learn from the situation and move on."	Frequency rating: ✓ or ✘: a b c d

Show strong commitment to meaningful objectives "I am able to discover what is meaningful to me in my life and I actively commit myself to pursuing these meaningful objectives."	Frequency rating: ✓ or ✗: a b c d
Develop discomfort tolerance "While I recognise that it is a struggle for me to tolerate discomfort, when it is in my interest to do so, I am able to tolerate it, I am willing to do so and I commit myself to doing so and remind myself I am worth doing all this for if I have any doubt about this."	Frequency rating: ✓ or ✗: a b c d
Adopt a balanced outlook on short-range hedonism and long-range hedonism "I recognise that it is important for me to strive towards important long-term goals while satisfying some of my short-term goals. I aim to keep a good balance between the two."	Frequency rating: ✓ or ✗: a b c d
Develop resilience "I recognise that I may buckle under the weight of adversity, but that I can recover, learn from the experience and gain greater strength and wisdom from doing so."	Frequency rating: ✓ or ✗: a b c d
Accept life unconditionally "I recognise that life is a very complex mixture of positive events, negative events and neutral events and choose to accept life unconditionally on this basis."	Frequency rating: ✓ or ✗: a b c d

20 healthy principles

Adopt a process view of life "I recognise that when I have achieved certain goals and objectives, this is not the end of the story. Once achieved, goals and objectives need to be maintained and even enhanced."	Frequency rating: ✓ or ✗: a b c d
Acquire a self-helping philosophy "While at times I need to rely on others to help me, by and large I am responsible for helping myself."	Frequency rating: ✓ or ✗: a b c d
Develop a problem-solving mindset "I see problems as challenges and believe that they are solvable. I have a sense that I have the ability to cope with problems and appreciate that this often involves time and effort. I also recognise that healthy negative emotions are an integral part of the overall problem-solving process that can ultimately be helpful in coping with these problems."	Frequency rating: ✓ or ✗: a b c d
Identify and use existing strengths and resources "I recognise that I have strengths that I can call upon both to help me deal with problems and to enhance my development. I also recognize that as I help myself, I can draw upon the resources that exist in the environment and those provided by others."	Frequency rating: ✓ or ✗: a b c d
Identify own values and base developing self on them "I recognise that I have several values that can guide me as I strive to develop myself. I can identify these and learn to operationalise them."	Frequency rating: ✓ or ✗: a b c d

Other principles (list below) **1.**	Frequency rating: ✓ or ✗:
2.	Frequency rating: ✓ or ✗:
3.	Frequency rating: ✓ or ✗:

© Windy Dryden, 2017

Notes

Introduction

1 In this book, I will use the term 'objectives' to refer to what coachees want to achieve from development-focused REBC and the term 'goals' to refer to what coachees want to achieve from problem-focused REBC.
2 While the word 'should' in REBC theory may indicate the presence of a rigid and extreme attitude, in this book it will mainly be used in its recommendatory form, unless otherwise indicated. Thus, when I say that REB coaches 'should' follow the steps outlined in this book, I mean that I recommend that they do so, not that they absolutely have to do so. Coaching steps 'should' be used flexibly, not rigidly.

Chapter 1: Laying the foundations (LTF): Helping coachees to get the most from REBC

1 I am aware that some coaches only work via Skype or such platforms, in which case the assessment session would be via such platforms.
2 A coaching contract covers a range of coaching and practical issues that will not be discussed here; see Dryden (2017).

Chapter 2: A step-based framework for the practice of emotional problem-focused REBC (EPF-REBC)

1 I am beginning with a step-based framework for the practice of EPF-REBC because these steps are also relevant when dealing with emotionally based obstacles to coachee progress in all types of REBC.
2 Bernard (2018b) refers to such obstacles as "psychological blockers to successful coaching outcome."
3 The illustrative case material is shown in italics.
4 In REBC theory, UNEs are clearly differentiated from HNEs. The former are problematic or disturbed responses to adversities at 'A' that give rise to

coachees seeking help. The latter are realistic and constructive responses to the same adversities. As can be seen, what sets these two types of emotions apart is their healthiness, not their negative feeling tone. Thus, according to REBC theory, it is healthy to feel bad (but not disturbed) about an adversity. Some REB coaches use the terms 'disturbed emotions' and 'non-disturbed emotions' to refer to UNEs and HNEs, respectively, but in this book, I will use the latter terminology.

5 See Dryden (2017) for a fuller discussion of the differences between UNEs and HNEs and how to use this distinction in emotional problem-focused coaching.
6 The phrase 'dialectical engagement' usually refers to a discourse between two or more people holding different points of view about a subject but wishing to establish the truth through reasoned arguments. I have adapted the use of this term to the situation in coaching whereby one person (i.e. the coachee) holds opposing attitudes towards an adversity and wishes to establish, again through reasoned argument, which attitude is truthful, most sensible and most helpful and which is false, least sensible and least helpful.
7 I will illustrate these standpoints by using the method where rigid and extreme attitudes and flexible and non-extreme attitudes are questioned at the same time.
8 From the song 'Teach Your Children' by Crosby, Stills and Nash.
9 What I have to say in this section also applies to dealing with obstacles in the other two types of coaching that are the focus of this book. While I will focus on EPF-REBC here, please extrapolate to practical problem-focused REBC and development-focused REBC.
10 The term 'meta-EP' means having an emotional problem about an emotional problem.

Chapter 4: A step-based framework for the practice of development-focused REBC (DF-REBC)

1 Bernard (2018a) refers to these as "rational principles of living."
2 Albert Ellis (1913–2007) was the founder of Rational Emotive Behavior Therapy. Although Ellis did not specifically write on coaching, his ideas on how humans can live psychologically healthy and happy lives form the backbone of REBC as described in this chapter and in this volume.
3 Let me remind you that, in this book, I have decided to use term 'objectives' to refer to what coachees want to achieve from DF-REBC and the term 'goals' to refer to what coachees want to achieve from PF-REBC.
4 In doing so, I am not suggesting that a coach will implement all strategies for all coachees. Rather, I suggest that the coach employs a particular strategy that is salient for a particular coachee.

5 A stakeholder is anyone in addition to the coach and the coachee who has an interest in the coaching that occurs in the coaching relationship.
6 In my view, it is important for the coach to take such a test themself to determine its face validity before suggesting that their coachee completes it. I have done this test myself and concluded that it did accurately portray my values in rank order.
7 When I was growing up, there was no cod liver oil in capsule form, only in liquid form, which is very unpleasant. While we did not dispute its health benefits, we dreaded the call to "open your mouth and don't make a fuss" as we swallowed the foul-tasting stuff. If we were lucky, we were given a chocolate to take the taste away.

References

Bernard, M.E. (2011). *Rationality and the Pursuit of Happiness. The Legacy of Albert Ellis*. Chichester: Wiley-Blackwell.

Bernard, M.E. (2018a). Rationality in coaching. In M.E. Bernard & O. David (Eds.), *Coaching Reason, Emotion and Behavior Change: Rational-Emotive, Cognitive-Behavioral Practices*. New York: Springer.

Bernard, M.E. (2018b). Psychological blockers to successful coaching outcomes: A rational-emotive, cognitive-behavioral analysis. In M.E. Bernard & O. David (Eds.), *Coaching Reason, Emotion and Behavior Change: Rational-Emotive, Cognitive-Behavioral Practices*. New York: Springer.

Bernard, M.E. & David, O. (Eds.) (2018). *Coaching Reason, Emotion and Behavior Change: Rational-Emotive, Cognitive-Behavioral Practices*. New York: Springer.

Carter, A. (2006). *Practical Methods for Evaluating Coaching*. Brighton: Institute for Employment Studies.

Cavanagh, M.J. (2005). Mental-health issues and challenging coachees in executive coaching. In M.J. Cavanagh, A.M. Grant & T. Kemp (Eds.), *Evidence-Based Coaching: Theory, Research and Practice from the Behavioural Sciences* (pp. 21–36). Bowen Hills: Australian Academic Press.

David, O., David, D. & Razvan, P. (2018). Evidence-based coaching. In M.E. Bernard & O. David (Eds.), *Coaching Reason, Emotion and Behavior Change: Rational-Emotive, Cognitive-Behavioral Practices*. New York: Springer.

DiGiuseppe, R. (1991). Comprehensive cognitive disputing in rational-emotive therapy. In M. Bernard (Ed.), *Using Rational-Emotive Therapy Effectively* (pp. 173–195). New York: Plenum.

Dryden, W. (1985). Challenging but not overwhelming: A compromise in negotiating homework assignments. *British Journal of Cognitive Psychotherapy*, 3, 77–80.

Dryden, W. (2017). *Cognitive-Emotive-Behavioural Coaching: A Flexible and Pluralistic Approach*. Abingdon: Routledge.

References

Dryden, W. & Branch, R. (2008). *The Fundamentals of Rational Emotive Behaviour Therapy: A Training Handbook*. 2nd edition. Chichester: Wiley.

Ellis, A. (1963). Toward a more precise definition of 'emotional' and 'intellectual' insight. *Psychological Reports*, 13, 125–126.

Gessnitzer, S. & Kauffeld, S. (2015). The working alliance in coaching: Why behaviour is the key to success. *The Journal of Applied Behavioural Science*, 51, 177–197.

Gray, D.E. (2004). Principles and processes in coaching evaluation. *International Journal of Mentoring and Coaching* 2. Online at: www.emccouncil.org/uk/journal.htm.

Iveson, C., George, E. & Ratner, H. (2012). *Brief Coaching: A Solution-Focused Approach*. Hove: Routledge.

Kazantzis, N., Whittington, C. & Dattilio, F. (2010). Meta-analysis of homework effects in cognitive and behavioral therapy: A replication and extension. *Clinical Psychology: Science and Practice*, 17, 144–156.

Lazarus, A.A. (1993). Tailoring the therapeutic relationship, or being an authentic chameleon. *Psychotherapy: Theory, Research & Practice*, 30, 404–407.

Palmer, S. (2008). The PRACTICE model of coaching: Towards a solution-focused approach. *Coaching Psychology International*, 1, 4–6.

Wildflower, L. (2013). *The Hidden History of Coaching*. Maidenhead: Open University Press.

Index

Note: page references in *italic* refer to figures, those in **bold** refer to tables

action plans 47–51
adversity/adversities 5, 6, *11*, 13, 14, 15, 16, 22–27, 29; *see also* emotional problems; obstacles; practical problems
applicants 2–3, 4–7; *see also* coachees
assessment 2–3, **3–4**, 4–7
attitudes 18–20, 21; extreme 6, *11*, 13, 16, 18, 21; flexible 6, *11*, 14, 16, 18, 19, 21–22; non-extreme 6, *11*, 14, 16, 18, 19, 21–22; rigid 6, *11*, 13, 16, 18, 19, 21; *see also* 'Windy's Review Assessment Procedure'

Bernard, M.E. 6, 43
brainstorming 37

Cavanagh, M.J. 5
coachees 1, 6; end of coaching process 54–55; evaluation 7, 42, 55, 56, **57–58**, 58; follow-up 55–56, 58; resources 8, 35, 49; strengths 7–8, 35, 49
coaches *see* REB coaches
coaching contracts 2, 7, 31, 49, 54
coaching process: end of 54–55; evaluation 7, 55, 56, **57–58**, 58; follow-up 55–56, 58

development-focused REBC (DF-REBC) 1, 5, 6, 31, 43, 47; action plans 47–51; generalisation 52–53; healthy principles of living 43–44, 45, 47, 50–51, 53, 60–65; mediators 44, 50; objectives 1, 6, 44, 45–49, 50–53
dialectical engagement 18–20, 21
DiGiuseppe, R. 19, 20
doubts, reservations and objections (DROs) 21

Ellis, A. 19, 43
emotional problem-focused REBC (EPF-REBC) 5, 6, 9–13, 14–16, 26–28, 31, 43; attitudes 21–22; dialectical engagement 19–20, 21; generalisation 27–28; goals 6, 15, 18; healthy negative emotions 15, 18; homework tasks 22–26; obstacles 28–30, 40; persuasive arguments 20–21; 'PRACTICE' framework 29–30, 32, **33**, 35, 36; 'Situational ABCDEFG' framework 10, *11*, 13, 16, 19, 22, 26–27, 29; Target EP 9–12, 13, 15, 16; unhealthy negative emotions 11–13; Windy's Magic Question 13, **14**; 'Windy's Review Assessment Procedure' 16, **17–18**
emotional problems (EP) 1, 5, 6, 9, 10, 29, 30, 31, 34, 43
enquirers 2–3, 4–7; *see also* coachees

EPF-REBC *see* emotional problem-focused REBC
evaluation 7, 42, 55, 56, **57–58**, 58
extreme attitudes 6, *11*, 13, 16, 18, 21; *see also* 'Windy's Review Assessment Procedure'

face-to-face assessment 2, 3, 4, 6–7
feedback 7, 54–56, **57–58**, 58
flexible attitudes 6, *11*, 14, 16, 18, 19, 21–22; *see also* 'Windy's Review Assessment Procedure'
follow-up 55–56, 58

generalisation 27–28, 52–53
goals 6, 15, 18, 35–36

healthy negative emotions (HNE) 15, 18, 34
healthy principles of living 6, 43, 55, 56; development-focused REBC 43–44, 45, 47, 50–51, 53, 60–65
homework tasks 22–26, 40

inference 11, 12, 26

James (example) 34, 36, 37, 39–40, 41, 42

mediators 44, 50
'meta-EP' 30

negative emotions: healthy 15, 18, 34; unhealthy 11–13, 34
non-extreme attitudes 6, *11*, 14, 16, 18, 19, 21–22; *see also* 'Windy's Review Assessment Procedure'

objectives 1, 6, 44, 45–49, 50–53
obstacles 1, 6, 7, 24, 28–30, 41

Palmer, S. 32
persuasive arguments 20–21
potential solutions 36–41, 42
practical problem-focused coaching (PPF-REBC) 1, 5, 6–7, 32; brainstorming 37; emotional problems 34; goals 35–36; obstacles 41; potential solutions 36–41, 42; problem identification 32–34
practical problems (PP) 1, 5, 6–7, 29–30, 32–34; potential solutions 36–41, 42
'PRACTICE' framework 29–30, 32, **33**, 35, 36
pre-assessment coaching questionnaire 3, **3–4**, 7
problem-focused coaching (PF-REBC) *see* emotional problem-focused REBC; practical problem-focused REBC
problem identification 32–34
problem-solving 6, 32, 36–41, 42; *see also* 'PRACTICE' framework; 'Situational ABCDEFG' framework

Rational Emotive Behavioural Coaching (REBC) 1, 6, 7; *see also* coachees; coaching process; REB coaches
rational principles of living *see* healthy principles of living
REB coaches 1–3, 4–8, 10, 20, 32; end of coaching process 54–55; evaluation 7, 42, 55, 56, **57–58**, 58; follow-up 55–56, 58
REBC theory 14
resources 8, 35, 49
rigid attitudes 6, *11*, 13, 16, 18, 19, 21; *see also* 'Windy's Review Assessment Procedure'
risk-taking 44, 50

Sarah (example): development-focused REBC 45, 48, 50, 51, 52, 53, 58–59; emotional problem-focused REBC 9, 10, 11, 12, 13, 16, 21, 24, 26, 27–28, 30, 31
'Situational ABCDEFG' framework 10, *11*, 13, 16, 19, 22, 26–27, 29

'SMART' (specific, measurable, achievable, relevant, time-bound) 35
strengths 7–8, 35, 49

Target EP (TEP) 9–12, 13, 15, 16
'teach your children well' technique 21

unhealthy negative emotions (UNE) 11–13, 34

Windy's Magic Question 13, **14**
'Windy's Review Assessment Procedure' (WRAP) 16, **17–18**

Taylor & Francis eBooks

Helping you to choose the right eBooks for your Library

Add Routledge titles to your library's digital collection today. Taylor and Francis ebooks contains over 50,000 titles in the Humanities, Social Sciences, Behavioural Sciences, Built Environment and Law.

Choose from a range of subject packages or create your own!

Benefits for you
- Free MARC records
- COUNTER-compliant usage statistics
- Flexible purchase and pricing options
- All titles DRM-free.

Benefits for your user
- Off-site, anytime access via Athens or referring URL
- Print or copy pages or chapters
- Full content search
- Bookmark, highlight and annotate text
- Access to thousands of pages of quality research at the click of a button.

REQUEST YOUR FREE INSTITUTIONAL TRIAL TODAY

Free Trials Available We offer free trials to qualifying academic, corporate and government customers.

eCollections – Choose from over 30 subject eCollections, including:

Archaeology	Language Learning
Architecture	Law
Asian Studies	Literature
Business & Management	Media & Communication
Classical Studies	Middle East Studies
Construction	Music
Creative & Media Arts	Philosophy
Criminology & Criminal Justice	Planning
Economics	Politics
Education	Psychology & Mental Health
Energy	Religion
Engineering	Security
English Language & Linguistics	Social Work
Environment & Sustainability	Sociology
Geography	Sport
Health Studies	Theatre & Performance
History	Tourism, Hospitality & Events

For more information, pricing enquiries or to order a free trial, please contact your local sales team: www.tandfebooks.com/page/sales

 The home of Routledge books

www.tandfebooks.com